THE TRAVEL MOM'S

Ultimate Book of Family Travel

THE TRAVEL MOM'S

Ultimate Book of Family Travel

Planning, Surviving, and *Enjoying*

Your Vacation Together

EMILY KAUFMAN

Broadway Books • New York

PRINTED IN THE UNITED STATES OF AMERICA

Visit our Web site at www.broadwaybooks.com

First Edition

Book design by Judith Stagnitto Abbate/Abbate Design

Library of Congress Cataloging-in-Publication Data
Kaufman, Emily.
The travel mom's ultimate book of family travel : planning, surviving, and
enjoying your vacation together / Emily Kaufman.—1st ed.
p. cm.
1. Travel. 2. Family recreation. 3. Vacations. I. Title.
G151.K37   2006
790.1—dc22   2005050745

ISBN 0-7679-2063-5

1   3   5   7   9   10   8   6   4   2

This book is dedicated to the most wonderful
traveling companions a mom could wish for—
my son, Charlie, my daughter, Gabby, and
my husband, Sid. I simply could not be
the Travel Mom without them.

Contents

Acknowledgments

There are so many people who have helped me to make the dream of writing this book a reality. My amazing agents, Kathleen Spinelli and Robert Allen, guide me through the publishing world and make me feel completely secure in uncharted waters. Billie Fitzpatrick was sent to me from the gods of writing, and I am grateful for her collaborative energy and enthusiasm. Patricia Medved at Broadway Books is a fellow traveling mom, and I am so thankful for her belief in me and my project. The many publicity professionals with whom I have the pleasure of working with every day are incredibly important to me, and I treasure these relationships. My friend Julie Carruthers has supported me as the Travel Mom from day one, and I know that she has believed that I could do this from the start. Now that my kids are teenagers, I look forward to traveling the world with my sister Stephanie, her husband, Mike, and their two fabulous angels, Carly and Josie. My biggest fan has been and continues to be my husband, Sid, and I am so lucky to be married to a man who supports me the way he does.

Introduction

Family vacations are the source of some of our most cherished family memories. From the first camping trip, to the first visit to Disney World, to a magical return to a favorite beach resort, vacations spent with our kids present us with special time together when our normal routines don't hamper or distract us. Family vacations also offer a magnificent opportunity to experience and explore different cultures, learn something new, and inspire kids with a thirst for the world. And though we often have wonderful intentions about what vacations are supposed to do for us as families, it's very easy for us to become overwhelmed as soon as we begin trying to turn our vacation dreams into a reality.

Our worries usually begin when we contemplate just how to pay for a vacation. "How can we afford a vacation?" "Sorry, dear, we just don't have much room in the budget for a vacation this year." As family purse strings tighten and travel prices rise, it's become more difficult to plan an affordable family vacation. But it's not impossible. Though many travel destinations are pricey, it's absolutely possible to plan a trip that stays within a set limit and offers you and your family an opportunity to rest, relax, and have fun!

We've all heard, and have also asked ourselves, that backseat standard "Are we there yet?" Why do we tend to begin our vacations in impatience and frustration?

"I'm bored!" is, unfortunately, another vacation nightmare phrase. So much energy, time, money, and emotion are involved with planning a family vacation that this one sentence can send even the most patient mom into a frenzy.

You've probably already realized that it usually falls upon Mom to satisfy the needs of many, keep the peace, and stick to a budget. So how do you plan a vacation that is truly enjoyable for everyone, including yourself?

I hope to provide the answer in this book. I have collected practical information to show you how to plan that dream vacation you may already have in mind, and I can also give you ideas about vacations in fabulous, over-the-top destinations. Since becoming the official Travel Mom and launching my Web site about a decade ago, I have spent most of my life on planes and trains and in automobiles, figuring out how to make traveling with kids more enjoyable and less stressful. I have been lucky enough to learn the ins and outs of planning the best vacation possible. Now I want to help you do the same.

About nine years ago, after having worked as a parenting and family expert for more than fifteen years, I realized that the travel industry needed a voice to speak directly to people interested in family travel—people like me and you. Indeed, my family—my husband, Sid, my son, Charlie, fifteen, and daughter, Gabby, thirteen—has always been a group of enthusiastic travelers. And yet when we began traveling as a family, there were no signposts out there leading us away from big mistakes such as overpacking, choosing a resort that didn't cater to kids, selecting a restaurant that didn't have a children's menu, or overscheduling our time away. Now, more than a hundred trips later, I feel quite confident in all I have to share with you about what to do and what not to do when traveling with kids, no matter what age they are.

We've all had at least one of those trips that seem to start in a haze of chaos and never recover. Here you will find hundreds of easy-to-implement tips that can get your vacation off to its best start—and ending! It is my mission to give you advice and insight on how you can plan the vacation of your dreams: one that brings the family together rather than tears it apart.

Whether you know exactly where you want to go or need help coming up with the perfect destination for your family, *The Travel Mom's Ultimate Book of Family Travel* will take the aggravation out and put the pleasure into your vacation. Part 1 focuses on helping you decide how, when, and where you want to go and gets you started selecting, planning, and arranging for your trip. The planning chapter shows you how to determine a budget, choose a destination, and gather information about your hotel or resort and the accommodations, amenities, and services it offers. You will also find helpful hints on what to expect when traveling by air, train, or car in this age of high security, high gas prices, and highly demanding children!

For those who want to vacation with their extended family, an entire chapter is devoted to strategies for multigenerational travel, including tips on how best to get along when relatives are together! There is also a chapter on how to give your children educational experiences without their realizing it. And though I don't recommend ever advertising to your kids that a trip is "educational," there are many ways to open their eyes, engage their minds, and inspire their hearts through travel. With that in mind, I have gathered a list of my favorite museums, historical sites, and points of cultural interest that will excite even the most boredom-prone child.

Throughout, you will also find other practical information to make traveling easier, including great Internet sites that cater to planning your trips, finding accommodations, and learning about activities in your destination.

Part 2 is devoted to the best of the best Travel Mom destinations. For those of you who already know what kind of trip you want to take or who have traveled with your kids extensively, you may want to skip right to Part 2 so you can select your destination from among the hundreds that I describe. Although I focus mostly on destinations within the United States, the Caribbean, and Canada, you will find a few mentions of locations outside North America, including a trip to London. The destinations include suggestions for beach vacations (Chapter 5), winter travel trips (Chapter 6), alluring all-inclusive resorts (Chapter 7), the increasingly popular family cruises (Chapter 8), soft adventures for families who like a bit of action and some outdoor challenges (Chapter 9), campsites across the U.S. (Chapter 10), great cities to visit with kids (Chapter 11), and finally, my hidden treasures (Chapter 12), those easy-to-find but easy-to-miss gems that are just outside the travel radar.

Each destination chapter also contains a "once in a lifetime" trip. These trips are special not only because they require more planning and more money and are usually a greater distance to travel, but also because they tend to create family memories that will last a lifetime. Vacations offer unique opportunities to seal these moments for families forever. Over the years, I have experienced a number of what I call "Golden Moments." These are times when my family was all around me, the setting was spectacular and unique, and I was present in all ways. Golden Moments always bring me to tears—of pleasure, joy, and gratefulness. To me, this should be everyone's goal while on vacation with her family. And it's not so impossible to realize such a dream. In fact, as I kept thinking about what all my Golden Moments had in common, I realized that certain conditions were always present. I have recorded the conditions for creating these special, never-to-be-forgotten memories in the Travel Mom's Twelve Golden Moment Rules.

Rule #1   Don't Overschedule

Rule #2   Leave Work at Home

Rule #3   Take a Deep Breath!

In our most calm, collected moments, we dream of our family vacations as blissful bonding experiences. We imagine our family spending time together with everyone enjoying one another's company and creating wonderful memories that are recorded in photo albums, scrapbooks, and home videos. And, snap! This idea can disappear in one instant with the first argument between the kids, a toddler's meltdown, or your own exhaustion. The reality of relationships, children being off schedule and away from the security of home and routine, and the inevitable hassles and blips when on the road or in the air can make travel and being on vacation trying, to say the least.

So how does everyone have fun and stay sane at the same time?

I'm realistic when it comes to family vacations. I don't like to pretend that all will be bliss—it never is at home. Why would our traveling to another place erase all family squabbles and differences? With this reality in mind, I always establish three main goals for vacations spent with my family:

1. There should be a few planned activities that we can do together as a family.
2. Flexibility will be allowed for everyone to do his or her own thing at least once, if not more.
3. There will be time set aside to spend with just my husband.

The first goal may seem obvious, but many families overlook how family activities accomplish two things at once: keeping your kids busy and entertained and giving you all the chance to be together and bond as a family. Many resorts and destinations offer interesting, fun, and challenging activities that families can do together—whether it be a daylong bike trip, white-water rafting, or a simple hike and picnic. So once you have decided on your destination, look into what activities of interest are available and/or suitable for your family, and plan ahead.

The second goal comes from my belief that everyone needs time alone to do whatever he or she wants: relax, sleep, read, play sports, find thrills. On vacation, I love to indulge in the luxury of a long nap. My husband brings along all his magazines that he hasn't had a chance to read in the preceding months. And my kids just do their own thing. Obviously, you can't send your toddlers off on their own, but you and your partner can alternate supervising them, giving each other some quality time alone. Encouraging everyone to spend time alone gives the group a breather and helps diffuse the natural tension that comes from being in a strange place and off routine. Then when everyone rejoins—say, at the end of the day or at dinner in the evening—there is more joy and positive energy. The group has been refreshed.

The third goal is a must for couples. Haven't we all listened to exhausted friends return from a family vacation wanting their kids to disappear or be sent to work camp in Siberia? You can hear the frustration in their voices as they complain about how they didn't get any rest on vacation, that the vacation was all about the kids, and that now they are not even speaking to their husbands!

This situation can and should be avoided. Depending on your destination or type of vacation, many resorts are available that offer organized children's activities, babysitting, and other ways to occupy your kids. Take advantage of these opportunities and plan some intimate time with your partner. And don't feel guilty. Many working parents, anxious to spend quality time with their kids on vacation, forgo putting aside time for themselves. In the end, everyone suffers. It's as important to give yourselves relaxing time away from your kids as it is to spend time with them.

But don't wait until you arrive to start planning. You need to make calls ahead of time so you know exactly what kind of coverage you can get while you're on vacation and make reservations if necessary. You should also verify that the caregivers, camp counselors, or other people who will be supervising children are given background checks or training. This will make you rest easier when your kids are out of your sight.

Remember, if you don't schedule certain things, they just don't happen. It's just as important to earmark vacation time for fortifying your relationship with your partner as it is to set aside time for bonding with your children.

Here are some ideas that might spark inspiration or desire:

- Go for a long stroll on the beach together.

- Go to dinner—just the two of you.

- Plan an activity that just you and your partner participate in—tennis, golf, skiing, or even shopping.

- Sleep in and let the kids fend for themselves in the early part of the day.

- Stay up late—after the kids have finally gone to sleep—and rent an old movie or play cards.

I hope these ideas inspire, challenge, and comfort you as you and your family discover years of vacation dreams together. This book is for all of you parents out there who are determined to have a nice time on vacation—after all, not only is it possible, but it's your right. Now go for it!

· PART ONE ·

Creating the
Family Vacation
of Your Dreams

· ONE ·

Planning Makes Perfect

We like to think that a good vacation is one that just happens, miraculously and serendipitously. We tend to imagine that planning might actually take away from the relaxing break from routine that vacation is supposed to represent. Nothing could be further from the truth.

Take this travel story. Trudy, Paul, and their two kids, Phoebe and Eric, wanted to take a break for a long weekend from their hectic, demanding lives in a busy suburb outside Chicago. It was late November; the warm months of summer were all but a distant memory and the cold midwestern winter was hunkering down for a long stay. Paul came home one evening from work and announced to Trudy and the kids that he had just bought four tickets on a discount airline to Florida.

Trudy said, "Where are we staying?" "I'm not sure yet," replied Paul. "We'll find something when we get there."

The family of four packed lightly and jumped on a flight to Florida the next morning. They arrived in the Fort Lauderdale airport to discover it overflowing with people. Trudy looked at Paul and said, "It's not even spring break. What's going on?"

They soon found out that there was an enormous convention taking place throughout the city. Not only were there no rental cars available, but there was barely a hotel room open. The dreamy long weekend of sun and fun that Paul had imagined had suddenly turned into a disaster.

How did this particular travel story end? The family ended up staying at a not-so-nice airport hotel and relying on expensive taxi rides to take them to the beach, shopping areas, and other tourist attractions. Phoebe and Eric were soon cranky and bored, and no amount of cajoling helped to lift their spirits.

By the time they returned home to Chicago, all they wanted to do was crawl into their comfortable beds.

Vacations-turned-nightmares are absolutely avoidable if you follow one simple rule: Plan your vacation. Yes, it does take time and focus to plan a good vacation, but that effort always brings its rewards—and this is especially true when planning a vacation with your children. Gone are the days of packing a simple overnight bag with your partner and jumping on a plane out of town. With children in tow—whether those kids are toddlers or teenagers—it is absolutely essential that you take steps to plan your vacation in order to maximize your enjoyment and minimize your discomfort. Planning also ensures getting the most out of your travel dollar.

What does planning encompass?

Define Your Travel Experience

Now it's time to get started. I suggest, at the risk of sounding corny, sitting in a quiet place and trying to visualize how you want to *feel* on your vacation. What kind of a vacation *experience* are you looking for? This decision can feel overwhelming and confusing, even for the most well-traveled person or family. I have developed a short work sheet for helping you determine what kind of trip you want to take, where you want to take that trip, how much you want to or can spend on such a trip, and when you want to go. You may know the answers to most or all of these questions. Fine. Simply use the work sheet to assemble your information in a clear, concise way, which will help you begin to plan and organize.

How much mental stimulation do you want? Are you looking for sun or snowy cold? Do you want to be physically active or no? These are basic but important questions that will help you achieve your vacation dream and avoid having an experience that no one really planned on having—I call this the vacation regrets—which too often means that you end up returning home more exhausted than when you left and need a vacation to recover from your vacation. Yikes!

I advise that you sit down with a clean sheet of paper or blank computer screen and read through and answer the questions below. As you do so, you will begin the selection process.

Vacation Planning Work Sheet

1. What is your travel mood: energetic, quiet, or a mix of the two?

2. Do you want to visit a warm or cold climate, or does it matter?

3. Do you and your family enjoy doing a lot of activities, such as sightseeing or touring? Or do you want to spend time primarily resting?

4. Do you and your family enjoy the outdoors, or do you prefer full amenities?

5. Do you already know your dates of travel? With school schedules, many families know well in advance when they are taking vacation. If you know your dates, you have valuable information for determining the costs, availability, and other details about your trip. If you have more flexibility around when you can travel, seasons often help determine the type of trip. If it's February and the days are cold and short, you might be in the mood for a warm hiatus down south. If it's summertime, you may feel more up for an adventure. Then again, if it's winter and you and your family enjoy winter sports, you may want to consider a destination that provides such activities. (You will find specific destination suggestions in Part 2.)

6. How old are your kids, and do their ages preclude some trips? For example, if your kids are under five, then you probably do not want to plan a soft adventure in the outdoors. But if your kids are teenagers, they may want the thrill of a backroads experience. As you peruse the destinations in Part 2, keep in mind how your entire family can enjoy a particular trip.

7. Do you want to stay in a hotel, small inn, or bed-and-breakfast, or do you want to rent a condo or house? Your choice of accommodations in part depends on the ages of your children. If they are very young, then you may be more comfortable in a condo or house. Then again, you may want the services and amenities of a hotel or inn. (See more recommendations for choosing accommodations on page 19.)

8. What is your budget? It's important to decide beforehand exactly how much money you want to spend on your vacation. Determining this figure will help you narrow your field of options—regardless of how much or little you want to spend. Remember, no matter your budget, there is a perfect vacation for you. As you will see in Part 2, by choosing an all-inclusive resort or a cruise vacation, you can predetermine to the penny what you will spend, before you even leave your house!

9. Are you flexible enough to consider off-peak travel? All resorts, hotels, and packagers offer specials during off-peak times. Off-peak can mean midweek or off-season. So if you have flexibility with your vacation dates, then it is very well worth your while to find out rates during these off-peak times. You can receive a significant discount—and enjoy your vacation with a lot fewer crowds. This is true whether you're going north to snowboard or south to sunbathe or to a city to be a culture vulture for a week. But don't worry, if you have to travel during peak times (during holidays and summer vacation), there are plenty of ways to maximize your travel dollar and find added value. Keep reading!

After assembling all your information, you may still not know exactly where you want to go, but you are probably a lot closer to knowing how much you can spend, when you are traveling, and what type of vacation you want. Keep this information at hand as you continue the planning process. Sometimes narrowing your choices is hard because you want to do everything during one seven- or ten-day period. Try to remember that you can and will take many vacations in your lifetime, and that the one you are planning for now should fit your family now. If your family includes babies and toddlers, for example, it may be too soon to visit Disney World, and you might have a more relaxing and enjoyable time at an all-inclusive resort or on a cruise that provides babysitting and organized activities for toddlers. If your kids are no longer toddlers but are under twelve, then certain soft adventures may be too strenuous for them but perfect for when they turn fourteen. As you peruse the vacations described in Part 2, consider the ages and makeup of your family and let these factors help pare down your choices.

Choosing Your Destination

Perhaps your heart is set on taking your kids for a first-time trip to New York City. Or your family is gearing up for its first big trip to Disney World. Perhaps you and your family have decided to go as far away as Hawaii! In the chapters ahead, you will be able to gather more and more information about types of vacations—beach vacations, winter sport trips, cruises, extended visits to an all-inclusive resort or city, outdoor adventure trips, and meandering trips that include stops at some of America's hidden treasures. The more variety you see, the more likely you will be able to narrow your choices and come up with the perfect vacation plan for your family's next trip. It's also helpful in selecting a destination to ask your friends, extended family members, and coworkers where they have traveled and which places they have enjoyed as families. Word of mouth is always a great source of travel information.

To decide on your destination, use the selections described in Part 2 to begin your research. Here is a quick overview of the types of vacations described and their general locations:

- Beach vacations in and around New England, the mid-Atlantic states, the southern coast, the Gulf shore, the Great Lakes, California, and Hawaii

- Winter vacations in California, Colorado, Wyoming, Vermont, and Canada

- All-inclusive resorts in the Caribbean, Mexico, Colorado, Florida, and Bali

- Cruises through the islands of the Caribbean and Bahamas, and to Alaska

- Soft adventures such as white-water rafting, dude ranches, Outward Bound experiences, and BackRoad adventures

- Campsites across the U.S., including national parks

- Cities including New York, Boston, Philadelphia, Memphis, Chicago, Indianapolis, Los Angeles, Seattle, and London, England

- Hidden treasures in California, Canada, Hawaii, Florida, New York, Texas, Utah, and Wisconsin

If you are anxious to get started, by all means skip ahead to Part 2 and read through the specifics about all the destinations. No doubt, you will find at least one that matches all your criteria, and if you happen to find two or three that fit your desires or requirements, you can always take another vacation!

Getting Your Kids Involved

Should you get your kids involved in the decision-making process? That's a matter of both their age (they need to be at least six to have a logical opinion) and you and your parenting style. Do you typically invite your children to influence family decisions? Do you often ask them for their input when choosing a movie, deciding on dinner, or selecting their room color? If so, then it makes sense that you would ask your kids for their input on the type of vacation or its destination. On the other hand, if you and your partner make all family decisions, then your kids might be a bit perplexed if you suddenly ask them where they want to spend their spring vacation.

For those of you who want to include your kids in the decision, I will make one suggestion: Present your children with two or three possible options. There's very good reason behind this idea: Consider the havoc each morning at the breakfast table if you said, "Okay, kids, what do you want to have for breakfast?" Sally would say oatmeal, John would say pancakes, Hillary would say eggs, and Patricia would say waffles. You not only open the door to having to prepare four separate dishes, but you also create chaos that is certainly avoidable. Get the picture? Just as at mealtimes, you're in charge.

Incorporating the kids into the vacation-planning process is a sure-fire way to get them excited about where they will be going. Even more important, it may be a way to help improve their self-esteem. Kids have little control over what happens in their world on a day-to-day basis. So if you give them a chance to feel as though they have some investment in family decision-making, they come away with a greater sense of worth and the belief that their opinion matters.

Once the location has been determined, get the kids involved in the planning. The Internet is the perfect resource. Have your kids visit Web sites on the destination and take a look to see what interests them. Running a search through an engine like Google or Yahoo using the keywords of the place you are visiting can direct them to loads of great Web sites for fact-finding. And they can ask friends and relatives about the destination, too. You might want to give the kids a say about which amenities they would like when you are determining your accommodations, such as an arcade or a pool with a waterslide.

Consider allowing each of your kids to select one special activity that the family will participate in. Make sure that they understand that even if a specific activity that a sibling selects is not their favorite, they must participate with a good attitude, and everyone will do the same for them. If kids are given a little input into the vacation plans, they will feel a great sense of ownership.

You can also teach your kids some valuable lessons about budgets when planning a vacation. Many children have no idea how much it costs to visit a theme park or participate in other activities when they travel. I recommend setting a daily limit on your kids' spending and making sure they stick to it, with a firm cap on what they can spend. Some people I know encourage their children to earn money toward things they want to buy on vacation, but I prefer to give them a set amount and let them decide how to spend it. Souvenirs are included in this limit; you may want to discuss the idea of souvenirs before the trip begins, so you both clarify the kids' expectations (and spending) and prepare them for these limits.

Where You Lay Your Head— Lodging Tips and Suggestions

Keeping Within Your Budget

In general, for all types of destinations (beach, winter, all-inclusive, cruise, soft adventure, or hidden treasure), I have offered a selection from three main price-point categories: budget, moderate, and deluxe. Since the price of accommodations changes all the time, I have avoided naming exact costs. In order to best prepare your budget and choose your type of vacation, destination, and accommodations, you need to contact all resorts, hotels, or packagers for the most up-to-the-minute quotes.

As you use the three categories, you may want to consider these examples as guideposts:

Budget: *Motel 6, Econo Lodge*

Budget accommodations are clean and safe but include fewer amenities such as pools and restaurants. Their linens are fairly standard, their towels are on the small side, and the rooms generally lack individuality.

Moderate: *Holiday Inn, some Hiltons, and Embassy Suites*

This level of accommodations offers larger rooms, more comfortable linens, and some amenities such as pools and exercise rooms. The rooms are still fairly generic but often have good television and cable offerings, free Internet hook-up (as they cater to business travelers, too), and room service.

Deluxe: *Four Seasons or the Ritz-Carlton*

At this level the accommodations are luxurious, the room decor is specialized, the services are extensive, and the amenities are plentiful. Most hotels at this level offer pools, spas, and exercise facilities. The bed linens are fine, the rooms are spacious, and the restaurants and room service offer superior food.

Researching Your Options

Once you know your budget and destination, you are ready to select your accommodations. Here's my general advice and strategy for finding the right place to stay:

- Utilize an Internet search engine such as Travelocity, Orbitz, or Expedia to get a sense of the range of accommodations in the area of interest, and their location, amenities, and price points.

- If you already know the resort or hotel you want to stay at, contact it directly for rates, reservations, and specials. Do not assume the hotel agent will offer the information about specials; you must ask directly.

- If you've worked with a travel agent successfully in the past, contact him or her to see if the agent knows of any special deals at hotels or resorts in the city or town of your destination.

- Consider a vacation packager or tour operator, such as GoGo Worldwide Tours or Apple Vacations. A good way to find a tour operator is through the licensed United States Tour Operators Association (USTOA). Many of the airlines offer their own packagers, and you can find great deals on airline tickets, air transport, and hotel accommodations—especially for last-minute trips.

• Check out the vacation wholesalers, such as www.vacationoutlet.com, which offer incredible savings on packaged all-inclusive vacations. Restrictions and short notice usually apply.

• House or condo rentals—there are many good, reliable Web sites that offer rental houses or condos in vacation areas, such as the following:

www.cyberrentals.com

www.findvacationrentals.com

www.vacationhomes.com

www.A1vacations.com

www.valuevacationrentals.com

www.erhomes.com

www.vrbo.com

When it comes to sleeping accommodations, keeping to a budget does not mean you have to forfeit quality. With so many different places to go in the world, there's a lot of competition for vacationers, so when you plan your trip, be confident that you are in the driver's seat.

One thing that many people don't know is that you can almost always bargain a better price for a hotel room. Some people are not comfortable bargaining, but it doesn't need to be a production. You can simply ask either your travel agent or reservation clerk politely, "Do you have any specials this time of year?" Or, "That's a little bit more than my family had planned on spending, but we'd really like to stay at your hotel. Do you think you could offer me a lower rate?" Believe me, if the hotel is not fully booked, particularly if it's off-season, then you will probably get the discount. I know of a woman who stayed in five-star hotels all over Thailand for about forty dollars a night—she simply asked each time she booked a room if they could lower their price to match her budget. Now, obviously you're not going to be staying at the Ritz-Carlton for forty dollars a night, but there are definitely deals to be had. Hotels will negotiate to compete for your patronage.

Another consideration when you're booking your hotel room is its location. For example, just because you're going to Disney World doesn't mean you have to sleep in one of its on-site hotels, which can be pricey. If you're willing to stay at a hotel just a few minutes' drive from the theme park, you can often save up to 50 percent. You'll also find many fun options, including log cabins, fully stocked condos, and other inn- or motel-type accommodations.

Families with young children often prefer an apartment or condo situation to a hotel. Having access to a full kitchen allows mealtimes to be that much more comfortable and less expensive. And in general, condos or houses allow for more space, so while kids are napping, parents can relax in a separate room.

Most major resort areas also offer reasonably priced apartments, condos, townhouses, and single-family houses. Such home rentals—short-term or long-term—are a great way to stretch the travel dollar. Also, condos or rental houses usually come equipped with washer and dryer, dishwashers, and other amenities that families rely on. And, staying in a residential location often encourages you to get to know a city or town in a more intimate way. You and your family can spend the day visiting the area shops, walking around the sites, and enjoying the city like a local. This is particularly true of cities in which you do a lot of walking, such as New York and Boston. By renting an apartment, you can mingle with the locals and really enjoy a break from your routine. The downside to renting apartments or condos is they don't always include a pool, fitness center, any sort of maid service, or, of course, room service.

If your heart is set on a four-star hotel in your dream resort destination because you want to spend your vacation wining, dining, and being pampered, then I always say, "Go for it!"

Aside from learning about room rates and using an Internet search program (such as MapQuest) to see a hotel's exact location, here are some other questions you may want to pose when considering a hotel or resort:

- What is the atmosphere of the hotel: formal, casual, or thematic?
- Is the hotel in a city or rural location?
- How big are the rooms?
- How many rooms do I need?
- Does the hotel provide roll-away cots?
- Is there public transportation nearby?
- Does the hotel or resort offer any spa services?
- Is there a fitness center?
- Is there a business center or Internet access?
- What are the dining options?
- How convenient is the hotel to local attractions?

Allowing Enough Time and Last-Minute Travel Ideas

It's important to allow sufficient time to plan your vacation. For long vacations, I always try to allow between six and twelve months. A full year gives you plenty of time to make reservations at hotels or resorts, purchase air tickets, and make any other necessary arrangements. If you know your children's school vacation schedule or your partner's work schedule, arrange your travel dates in advance to get the best airfare rates, as well as the best choice for accommodations.

Yes, it's always better to plan your vacation, but in this fast-paced age of dual-income households in which one or both parents may travel for work, unexpected travel opportunities do pop up. How can you take advantage of a last-minute window to take your family on vacation? The good news is that there are some ways to find great deals at the last minute!

Virtually all the major airlines offer free memberships to online newsletters that post cut-rate airfare or prepackaged trips if you're willing to go at the last minute. For example, US Air's program, E-Savers, sends out e-mails to members each Wednesday, detailing flights at below-market cost to certain cities from your usual point of departure. As a member, you tell them the city you'll most likely fly out of, and they match that city with their routes.

A few great Web sites are geared to last-minute travel, including www.travelzoo.com. The first time you log on, you're asked to sign up for a free subscription and are then sent a weekly newsletter on the top twenty best last-minute travel deals. This site offers a range of deals, from four nights for the price of two at top-rated hotels, to highly discounted packages on cruises ($699) for a week! Check it out!

Arm Yourself with Information

Know thy place! This is my number-one travel mantra. Whether you research your vacation destination via the Internet, a travel guide, a travel agent, or resort brochures, it's your job to gather as much information about where you're going and staying *before* you leave. I cannot overestimate the importance of this step. That way you decide what you want to do and how to respond when plans begin to change. Remember my friends Paul and Trudy? They learned the hard way that you can't just wing it in this day and age of more complicated travel.

Another important reason to research your destination before your trip begins is to help prepare your kids for what to expect. This is especially crucial for young kids, who can get confused, disoriented, and downright fragile when taken out of their familiar surroundings and routines. Kids behave better when they are given some sense of what to expect. If you have sat down with your children, shown them the brochures of your destination, and talked about all the exciting adventures the family is about to embark upon, then they will be much more comfortable both en route and upon arrival.

As you research your destination, begin a running list of what activities (both outdoor and indoor), dining options, shopping sites, nighttime entertainment, kids' clubs or organized activities, and other recreation are available. Share this info with your kids and see if any one or two activities are an absolute "must do!" If an activity is popular, then it's often a good idea to reserve or make an appointment ahead of time. Most facilities have Web sites, 1-800 numbers, or at least a phone number so that you can set things up in advance.

Gathering information can also help you pack. If your resort has a fancy restaurant or your cruise has declared one evening "dress-up night," then you want to make sure you come prepared.

And finally, it's sometimes a bit intimidating to arrive in a place you've never been or to a resort or hotel that feels foreign. If you are already armed with information and have already asked most or all of your questions, then you will be much more confident about traveling outside your domain. A fantastic Web site, www.viator.com, lists activities, entertainment, lodging, dining, and other information for many cities and towns. Check it out as you begin planning your trip!

Map Out Your Time

Now that you have selected your destination, chosen your accommodations, and armed yourself with information, it's time to plan your days. If you're going on a beach vacation, keep in mind that someone may go a little stir crazy lying on the sand all day, and if it's one of your kids, this is a potential disaster. So, find out what Susie-itch can do besides lie on the beach. Can she take tennis or scuba diving lessons? Are there organized playgroups with other kids her age? If you're not sure, then call the hotel or resort where you're staying and ask them to help—that's what a concierge is for.

In general, you want to find out what types of activities are available. Here is a list of usual suspects:

- Activities that you can do with children or as families, including sports, crafts, or other recreation
- Tours to cultural or historical sites
- Visits to the theater, museums, or festivals
- Kids-only activities or clubs that offer organized and supervised activities for a set number of hours each day
- Spa services
- Shopping
- Nightlife and live entertainment
- Theme parks

I am a bit type A when it comes to organizing, and the clearest evidence of this is my passion for making lists. Just as I always arm myself with information, I always sit down and make lists of the possible options for excursions, tours, events, and places of interest. Next, I make a list of activities I think my family and I might enjoy. Again, the more you have thought about this beforehand, the more likely they will happen. I usually sit down with both of my kids, show them options of what's going on at a particular resort or in a particular city, and suggest they choose a couple of things they would really like to do while on vacation.

I then map out an activity for each day of the vacation. If you make a list like this, remember that it's not written in stone; rather, use it as a guide to get you up and out the door. If you all change your minds— for example, find yourselves not in the mood for a museum and would rather try a day at the local zoo—then you can consult your list of options. You should keep in mind rainy-day activities that are available in or near your resort, and I also suggest that you pack books, movies, and other things in which kids can immerse themselves during bad weather. With this strategy you can relax on your vacation instead of wasting time trying to figure out what to do each day.

Now, obviously the degree to which you need to plan in advance depends very much on the type of vacation you're taking. On a ski vacation, for example, your day is pretty much booked. The main things you would need to think about ahead of time would be signing up for lessons, clinics, or mountain-hopping excursions, investigating other winter sports such as snowshoeing, or going to a spa for a day.

Again, as you peruse the list of activities and venues that interest you, your partner, and your kids, consider any event that may require making a reservation or ticket purchase in advance.

The Pleasures and Perils of Packing, and Other Last-Minute Details

For me, packing used to be one of the most difficult travel tasks. I used to break out in a sweat each time I contemplated all that I might need while traveling. How would I survive without my favorite sweater or handbag, or my choice of all my T-shirts? Thankfully, those days are past. I now follow a simple, foolproof routine.

1. Plan an outfit for each day. This does not mean you or your children won't wear the same pants twice, but by thinking through

each day of the trip, you'll know how many outfits are truly necessary. By laying out a week's worth of outfits on your bed, you avoid overpacking, an absolute no-no!

2. Always, always bring your own toiletries. You want to bring personal stuff, from toothpaste, to dental floss, to a brush and comb, because this is the sort of thing that some resorts and hotels charge an arm and a leg for.

3. It's always a good idea to pack at least one sweater or light jacket—because even if you're going to the warmest place on earth, you will more than likely encounter a plane, train, bus, or hotel that keeps the air-conditioning at frigid temperatures.

4. Kids can get into messy trouble wherever they are, so while you definitely do not want to overpack, you do want to bring at least a few extra tops and bottoms in case your son's ice cream dribbles all over the jeans he was supposed to wear all week—because it will be a lot cheaper than having laundry service in a hotel. I always have an extra pair of undies and socks, too.

5. Remember that some nights you'll want to get a little dressy, so don't forget to pack at least one pretty dress for you, a nice outfit for your partner, and ditto for the children. Even if you're not sure you'll want to have any fancy dinners, I encourage you to bring at least one nice outfit for the troops, particularly if you're going on a cruise ship, where often there is a semiformal dress code for dinners.

6. Don't forget a mini first-aid kit: It's always good to have some rubbing alcohol, Band-Aids, antibiotic ointment, Imodium, Tylenol/ibuprofen, and a thermometer. I replenish the kit often. If anyone in your family takes prescription medicine, be sure to bring a copy of the prescription with you, as well as your insurance cards. And parents of young kids and babies may want to bring a commonsense parenting book for reminders on what to do when kids get sick.

Those with very small children—babes in arms—or who are traveling with an infant for the first time may want to consider bringing what you need in a carry-on. As Terry, mother of four-year-old Margaret and nine-month-old Emma, told me, "I learned the hard way. With my first daughter, I just winged it. I figured the hotel in the Caribbean would have everything—or access to everything—that I'd need. The trip turned out to be a disaster because they didn't carry the brand of formula I used at home, and the baby didn't eat for the first two days of the trip and barely slept for more than two hours at a time. By the third day, my husband and I just wanted to go home. This last trip, we went to the Bahamas, and I wasn't going to make the same mistake with my second daughter. I packed a small wheelie carry-on with all that I needed: jars of organic baby food, formula, some bottled water, and her cereal. I also packed the favorite foods of my older daughter, Margaret, who is still the quintessential picky eater. It was kind of a pain having an extra carry-on, but it saved me a world of worry. And when we arrived at our condo, we had everything we needed! We didn't have to worry about getting to the store right away. What a relief!"

Find out ahead of time if any of the major chain drugstores are in the area of your hotel or resort. Most U.S. destinations, especially in or near a major city, will have a chain drugstore or supermarket nearby, which can save you tons of packing worry and lugging around. You can buy jars of baby food, diapers, and other supplies, as well as other miscellaneous items that you might not find at home, such as water shoes for the young kids—they aren't always easy to find in Boston or New York in the middle of winter!

Some people also ship down necessary baby items, including both food and supplies like diapers and wipes, but this can be expensive—

especially if you are traveling outside the mainland United States. A service called JetSet Babies also can do all the worrying, packing, and shipping for you. If you want to forgo the hassle of bringing all your baby supplies and equipment with you, contact JetSetBabies.com fourteen days in advance of your arrival and have them arrange to send all that you need in terms of child care necessities—from diapers to bottles to medicine. This is a fabulous Web site geared for parents of young kids, filled with practical advice and links to other travel information. Another useful Web site, www.babiestravellite.com, helps families arrange travel accessories and supplies for babies and kids.

Whichever way you finally decide to handle packing for a baby, consider exactly what you need and find out in advance what is available and what's not. You know your kids, what they need, and what they can do without. Whether they're infants, toddlers, or middle schoolers, you don't want to be caught without a product that is absolutely necessary.

Another tip that makes for a smooth exit from home is to go through the following checklist a week or so before leaving on vacation:

- ❑ Have you put your mail on hold or asked a neighbor to collect it for you?
- ❑ Have you made arrangements for any pets well in advance?
- ❑ Have you put a temporary stop to your newspaper delivery?
- ❑ Have you arranged how you will get to the airport?

Last but not least, you may also want to think about how to prepare your kids for returning home once your vacation ends. Some families prefer to travel a day before they return to work or the kids return to school in order to give everyone time to unpack, unwind, and get back into their routine. Other families make sure they have an easy meal ready so no one has to run out to the store after arriving back home, tired from traveling. Many kids, especially those who are young, need

---

• *Golden Moment Rule #1* •

Don't Overschedule

*A*lthough the key to good planning is to research your options, gather information, and make some plans for what to do on vacation, it's also important to avoid overscheduling. Parents of young children usually are more aware that their babies, toddlers, and preschoolers need to rest or nap at least once during the day. But it's easy for parents to forget that tweeners and teenagers—and, yes, even adults—need to take time to do nothing. My family and I like to take power naps—ten or twenty minutes of lying down on the bed or sofa, closing our eyes, and letting our brains just stop. Naps such as these will leave you feeling not only refreshed but also reinvigorated for the rest of the day—or evening!

My advice: Take minibreaks throughout your trip so you continue to have the energy to enjoy being on vacation!

---

help transitioning back into their normal home life routine. To help buffer feelings of disappointment at returning to school or home, you may want to think about bringing back a small souvenir or memento such as a magnet, a shell, or a frame that captures the spirit of your trip. Once you arrive home, suggest that your child place the palm tree magnet on the fridge, for example, or do a crafts project painting the shells you collected together on the beach. This way the kids have a way of integrating their vacation into their home life.

Checklist for Planning

- ❑ Decide what kind of vacation mood you're in.
- ❑ Encourage your kids to get involved in choosing from two or

three possible types of vacations and then helping to research the destination.

❑ Gather information about your destination or resort.

❑ Plan a general list of all activities, events, and entertainment you would like to participate in.

❑ Make any necessary reservations or advance bookings.

❑ Pack wisely for climate, events, and venues.

❑ Make sure that each family member's carry-on includes all medical necessities, a change of clothes, and other must-haves.

❑ Make sure kids have their own entertainment in their carry-ons.

Despite your best efforts, even the best-laid plans can run amok. Your daughter may come down with a fever, your son may get sunburned to a crisp, or your darling husband may have eaten his way through a cruise and now is completely stopped up. Alas, they all will come crying to you. Anything and everything can put a wrench in a perfectly planned vacation. That's why it's important to keep in mind that, as much as you plan—and you know how I feel about planning—everything is not going to go exactly according to your original blueprint. Don't worry! These things happen. And since you have kids, you know that unexpected stuff is bound to pop up. So, give yourself some mental wiggle room, and keep your sense of humor. As one mother of six said to me, "You have to roll with the punches. That's life—on or off vacation!"

· TWO ·

Planes, Trains, and Automobiles

The Art of Getting from Here to There

It's taken you the requisite number of hours to pack everyone's essentials neatly into suitcases, you've suspended your newspaper delivery and contacted the post office to hold your mail, and the day has finally come to leave for your trip. Now all you have to do is get there.

Many people imagine that it's only when they arrive at their ultimate destination that their vacation really begins. This mind-set can set up everyone for disappointment. Why? Because you have not taken into account the "getting there" process. Whether you travel by air, land, or sea, it takes some know-how to turn travel time into a pleasurable experience instead of a relentless harangue of "Are we there yet?"

Let's face it: Traveling with one, two, or three or more children takes four arms, a strong stomach, and a cool head. So how can you minimize your discomfort, maximize your pleasure, and still arrive in one piece with all your luggage and paraphernalia in order to enjoy the *rest* of your vacation? Let's take a look.

A Road Trip State of Mind

Road trips are not just for Ken Kesey and his band of merry misfits. Since the 1950s, many families have created wonderful, lasting memories on trips they have taken in their cars. Of course, cars are now roomier than ever, with every conceivable amenity, from retractable cup holders to built-in DVD players. But I have found that it's not necessarily the amenities that make for a pleasurable road trip; it's your state of mind. Essentially, if you all pile into the car with the expectation that the trip is going to be long, boring, and uncomfortable, then it probably will be. On the other hand, if you plan ahead, bring some entertainment, and accept the fact that you will probably be in the car for a number of hours, then you stand a much better chance of enjoying rather than abhorring the travel time.

Here are some tips that have worked for me and my family, as well as many others:

As Always, Be Prepared

Being prepared for a road trip means outlining your route, getting the necessary directions, and calculating how long the trip will take you. Remember to utilize satellite direction programs such as MapQuest, OnStar, or other GPS systems if you are not sure of your route. And remember your cell phone and its in-car charger. If you don't have a car charger, get one!

Once you know the approximate mileage of the distance between your departure location and destination, then you can decide how many stops you probably will need and if you want to split the trip into one, two, or three days. Take a look at a map. Are there any interesting cities, towns, or sites on the way? You may enjoy stopping and discovering something new. Arm yourself with information beforehand about the various towns on your route to help you decide whether to stop or not. One of the Morrison family's most memorable trips occurred when they were driving from Houston to El Paso, Texas. Driving across Texas is not what you would call interesting—lots of desert, one-pump gas stations, and an occasional Denny's come to mind. But this time, they were looking at the map of Texas and decided it might be interesting to visit the Big Bend National Park. Situated in the southwest corner of Texas, Big Bend is a formidable terrain that abuts the Mexican border. Not always in the camping mood, Terry, the mom, agreed to take the detour because her husband and kids were so excited to see such rugged countryside. Not only did they get a taste of the Wild West, but they also learned a great deal about this state's history and its connection to Mexico. It was truly a memorable road trip for them.

MUST-HAVE CAR ITEMS

- Maps
- First-aid kit
- Motion-sickness medication
- Jumper cables
- Cell phone and charger
- Driver's license, car registration, and proof of insurance
- Travel potty
- Antibacterial wipes
- Boredom bags
- Snacks
- Water

If your destination is more than a day's drive, then it's a good idea to make a reservation ahead of time at a motel, hotel, or inn on the way.

Bring Boredom Bags

Boredom bags are my answer to "Are we there yet?" To make one, fill any bag, knapsack, or shoe box with your children's favorite diversions. I have also used cosmetic bags, which are handy because they zip. If your kids are young, then you will have to assemble the boredom bags for them, but most older kids like to fill their bags themselves. For them, suggest including puzzle books or regular books, and perhaps let each child select a brand-new book for the trip. Kids also like Magna Doodles, doodle pads, and Mad Libs books. Many school-age kids love to color and draw. Bring along a coloring book or pad of paper and a baggie of crayons, markers, or colored pencils. I also suggest some sort of tray or surface they can lean on—cookie sheets work great, and they work for magnetic toys and games. If kids are seated closely enough, they may even be able to play cards. If your children like to listen to music, suggest they bring their CD headset or MP3 player. If you have either a built-in DVD player or a small portable one, bring a selection of movies. Small children relax when they are watching something familiar—and you know how a four-year-old can enjoy her tenth viewing of *Finding Nemo*! Mariam, the mother of a three-and-a-half-year-old, also suggests bringing what she calls "long" movies and "short" movies. The short movies—twenty-five to thirty-five minutes long—often serve as a way for her daughter to relax before falling asleep in the car. Longer movies—those that run an hour or two—require keener attention.

If your kids have a LeapPad or Game Boy, make sure they include them in their boredom bags. I would be careful not to allow toys or objects that contain small parts that might fall into the seats or onto the floor of the car. I hate it when I have to unbuckle my seat belt again and again in order to help someone in the backseat retrieve a piece or part. Remember, kids in car seats have limited range!

Make technology your friend. Regardless of your rules at home for such electronic toys as Game Boys, portable DVD players, headphones, and the like, I encourage you to let your kids bring along their techno gear while traveling. First, they will be less likely to get bored and complain, and second, these important possessions will help put them at ease while traveling.

If you are not comfortable with your children watching movies in the car and would rather they read, bring books or books on tape to listen to. Kerry Fahey, the mother of three boys, ages eight, six, and two, told me that she and her family love to listen to mysteries on CD. When they took a family trip from Boston to Virginia last November, they listened to the first book of the Harry Potter series. And though Timmy, the two-year-old, couldn't quite follow the story, the rhythm of the voices lulled him into a nice two-hour nap!

It's fun for kids and parents to play games on the road. Many of us of a certain age no doubt remember long car rides without air-conditioning, stuck next to a sibling or two, with the only form of entertainment games we made up. I won't lecture you on the benefits of our kids using their imaginations, but I do insist on reminding you of some fun car games that still appeal to kids:

- The license plate game
- Campfire songs
- Ghost stories
- Aunt Susie's trunk—a memory game in which you pack the trunk with items from A to Z, remembering all the items that have been named before
- Cards—but remember that cookie sheet or tray!
- Pictionary

- Car bingo
- Brain Quest cards or other "question cards"

Spending time with your kids on the road doesn't have to be stressful or dull if you plan ahead, use some ingenuity, and don't forget those boredom bags!

Stretching Those Legs and Taking Care of Business

It's very important for your body and mind that you get fresh air, stretch, and move while traveling. Being cooped up in a car—even if your windows are down—can make you all restless and sleepy. Though you may not want to make frequent pit stops, encouraging everyone to get out of the car at a rest stop every few hours is a good idea. Again, if you've mapped out your route and have a sense of how long the trip should take, then you can also time rest stops. My family and I always bring along a soccer ball in the car so that when we make stops for gas we can kick the ball around, too. Also, keep your eyes peeled for a playground, or seek one out as you exit the highway. Letting the kids run free for fifteen or twenty minutes will do wonders for everyone's state of mind.

You may want to pack your lunch, or at least some snacks, beforehand. Food choices at rest stops along most highways are notorious for limited selections, most of it fast food.

For those of you traveling with small children, I recommend bringing a travel potty and wipes. This makes it easier to find places to stop for those little people with little bladders.

It's almost impossible to keep everyone calm and satisfied for the duration of a trip. Kids will fight, you and your partner will find something to argue about, and everyone will, at some point, begin to feel fatigued and irritable. Accept this, and take a break when you need to.

Basic Rules for a Good Road Trip

Some basic rules apply to planning a successful, enjoyable road trip:

- Gas up your car, and check the oil and tire pressure the day before the trip.

- Pack and load the car the night before your trip.

- Start at a reasonable time—which does not mean in the middle of the night, after dinner when everyone is tired and cranky, or too early in the morning.

- Make "getting there" part of the trip itself.

- Take frequent or as-needed breaks during the drive.

- Make sure to pack boredom bags—for the kids and you.

- Incorporate the road trip into your vacation by discovering a town, city, or hidden treasure (see Chapter 12 for ideas) along the way.

ROAD TRIP, ANYONE?

A great Web site for planning road trips and setting itineraries is www.randmcnally.com.

Up in the Air

In this age of heightened security, air travel has become even more of a challenge than just keeping your kids from tossing their toys—or their cookies—while in flight. Nowadays, it's necessary to arrive earlier for your flight so that you have adequate time to navigate the airport's security procedures, which many times include at least two long lines. Also, planes are often delayed, so air travel comes with extra waiting time at the airport. Traveling with children can make this process even more hair-raising.

Kids can become irritable, nervous, or downright scared going through airports and in flight. The heightened security since 9/11 has put many armed guards and officers in airports and also created much more detailed check-in procedures. I find it very helpful to prepare kids as much as possible for what to expect. Explain that the officers and guards are there for security, not because something is happening at the moment. Prepare your children for having to take off jackets and/or shoes, empty their pockets, and remove any jewelry that they may be wearing. Explain to younger kids that everything is all right and assure them that they are safe. By verbalizing this message, you calm them before they might become agitated by the process.

This kind of preparatory talk should also include discussion of how you expect them to behave once on the airplane. They need to know that airplanes are crowded and they should act accordingly: no loud talking, no walking or running in the aisle, and no kicking the chair back in front of their seat. It's important that kids learn the rules of etiquette as soon as they can understand—for their sake as well as everyone else's.

Some airports have children-designated waiting areas with toys. Otherwise, find an area where your family can "set up camp" while you wait for your flight. Encourage children to read a book, play with whatever is in their boredom bag, or walk around the airport with one another or one of their parents. Little ones love all the big windows and long corridors. In some big airports, such as Detroit, you can kill time by riding the monorails or intra-airport shuttles, and many airports have playgrounds, including Boston Logan's Kid Port, the observation gallery in Baltimore-Washington International Airport, Orlando International Airport's Child's Play Zone, and Chicago's Kids on the Fly.

If you already know that a child is afraid of flying, minimize his feelings of insecurity by encouraging him to bring a comfort object, such as a teddy bear, or something for entertainment, such as a book, headphones, or a portable DVD player. Obviously what a child brings is very individual.

Here are some quick tips to keep the stress level to a minimum:

- Equip each child with his or her own boredom bag. For air travel, it's best to use a knapsack. But remember not to make these bags heavy, or your little one will ask you to shoulder yet another piece of baggage.

- Pack a carry-on with a change of clothes for you and your kids.

- Bring toiletries and medicines with you in your carry-on.

- Pack snacks and/or a meal for you and the kids. Airlines today rarely offer meals for flights less than three hours long and their snack offerings are limited, so it's wise to bring your own snacks or meals for you and the kids. If traveling with infants or toddlers, make sure to bring food, bottles, and sippy cups with you.

- Bring along your child's favorite comfort item—blanket, teddy bear, or cushy pillow—which may encourage her to take a nap! But don't feel it's necessary to bring all ten toys she loves.

- If possible, bring along your car seat for your infant or toddler, especially if your child is used to sleeping in one. Again, this will encourage napping during the flight and also mean it's going to be there when you arrive, even if the rest of your luggage doesn't make it.

- Some young kids are sensitive to ascents and descents. It's recommended that infants drink (or suck) during takeoff and landing to minimize ear discomfort. Have older kids chew gum.

Ε-TICKETS

*A*lways make sure you print out your e-tickets at home before you go to the airport. This is a prudent precaution to avoid any hassles in the unlikely event that the airline somehow loses your seat; if you've ever been on a flight that's been overbooked, you know that this type of error is not unheard of. Plus, in these days of supertight security, an airline can arbitrarily demand that you have the printout or deny you access to the flight. Unlikely, but it can happen.

- Although airlines don't restrict adults from holding infants in their laps, the U.S. National Transportation Safety Board (NTSB) recommends that children under twenty pounds should be seated in rear-facing infant car seats, and children between twenty and forty pounds should be seated in forward-facing car seats.

Traveling by Train

In 1869, in Promontory, Utah, the nation celebrated when the last spike was driven into the Transcontinental Railroad. It's been a long while since then, but in an age of red-eye flights and Instant Messaging, maybe it's time to take a little time getting someplace. Rail travel has endured because traveling by train can be so pleasurable. Looking out the window at the passing countryside, the relaxing rhythm of the train, stretching your legs, grabbing a snack when hungry—all combine to make trains a wonderful way to reach your destination.

You can travel by train to and from most major cities. For example, if you are planning a trip to New York and decide to make a quick visit to Philadelphia, why not travel by train? If you're planning a ski vacation in Vermont, you can fly into New York and take Amtrak's "ski train" from New York's Penn Station to Burlington. Or if your family is planning a long trip to Disney World, you can board a train in Washington, D.C., and take your car with you!

It's always best to reserve seats in advance when traveling by train, and if you're traveling more than eight hours, I highly recommend booking a sleeper car for your family—it's more comfortable and private. Also, if your children are between the ages of two and fifteen, then they travel for half off the normal price of a ticket, and infants and toddlers travel free. (Note that Amtrak does not offer cribs for babies, so BYO or plan on sleeping with your bambino on one of the sleeper's bunk beds).

Do keep in mind that trains, even more so than planes, often have delays in schedules. Know the schedule beforehand, allow for time delays, and be familiar with public transportation options at your destination.

Your family might enjoy making a train trip a journey unto itself. Here are some of my favorite train trips:

• *Grand Canyon Railway*—This authentic steam train has been serving the route to and from the Grand Canyon for more than a century. Packages include overnight accommodations in Williams, Arizona, and at the Grand Canyon. Meals are also provided. Check out www.thetrain.com.

• *Civil War Sites*—Amtrak covers most of the country, with extensive rail lines up and down the East Coast, throughout the Midwest and California, and covering some of the South. One of my favorite trips takes you through the regions where the Civil War took place, from Atlanta to New Orleans. Authentic southern meals are prepared by chefs as you take in the sites of the battles between North and South. Contact www.amtrak.com.

• **American Orient Express**—This premier rail line offers luxurious trips in restored vintage trains, in which the journey becomes part of the destination. American Orient Express has a number of different itineraries, including trips to Copper Canyon and Colonial Mexico, El Paso, Chihuahua, Creel, Alamos, and Divisadero. Another trip winds its way through the antebellum South, stopping in New Orleans, Natchez, Savannah, Charleston, Charlottesville, and Washington, D.C. Or perhaps you want to see some of our national parks, including the Grand Canyon, Zion, Yellowstone, and the Grand Tetons. Elegant dining and wine service make this an upscale experience to remember. See www.americanorientexpress.com.

• **Trails and Rails**—Amtrak and the National Park Service have teamed up to provide a number of exciting train trips that incorporate stops at some of our country's most pristine national parks and monuments. The Sunset Limited travels between Del Rio and Alpine, Texas, and passes through the Amistad National Recreation area. The Southwest Chief travels between La Junta, Colorado, and Albuquerque, New Mexico, passing through Bent's Old Fort National Historic Site. The Heartland Flyer travels from Oklahoma City to Fort Worth, Texas, stopping at Chicksaw National Recreation Area, the Oklahoma City National Monument, and the Washita Battlefield. The Coast Starlight travels between Portland, Oregon, and Seattle, Washington, stopping at the Klondike Gold Rush National Historic Park. For more information about the Trails and Rails program, contact either www.nps.gov/trails&rails or www.amtrak.com.

Safety Issues While Traveling

It's always important to take precautions while traveling. No doubt, most of you follow these rules anyway, but I thought I'd remind you:

- Always wear seat belts—whether in the car or on a plane or train.

- Teach your kids how to cover a toilet seat with paper.

- Give kids instructions for if they get separated from you, and put important information, including your destination's address and phone number, and your cell phone number, on a card for them to keep with them at all times.

Checklist for Getting There

- ❑ Have you packed your essentials in a carry-on?
- ❑ Does everyone have his or her boredom bag?
- ❑ Does your carry-on or car contain a first-aid kit?
- ❑ Have you prepped the kids for the journey they are about to take?
- ❑ Have you researched any towns, cities, or hidden treasures along the way?

One more piece of advice—which applies both to traveling and to the vacation experience as a whole: Kids need routine. Traveling to your destination means suspending a child's regular routine. So don't be surprised if the eating is off, the nap is off, and the mood is off. Try to let it go. You will be able to fall into a groove once you arrive. At the same time, once you do arrive at your destination, try to emphasize as much as your child's routine as possible. If bedtime is always bath, story, bed—then it's still bath, story, bed on vacation. You may be in a different place and a different time zone, but routine gives kids comfort. It's up to you to find the line between being flexible (for example, on vacation, bedtime might be later) and setting up some parameters.

• *Golden Moment Rule #2* •

Leave Work at Home

*T*he first way you can prepare for your vacation is to clear your mind and leave your work at home. I know, I know: with e-mail, voice mail, and now BlackBerries, no one at the office believes that you are out of reach. But don't leave your access up to your boss or coworkers. Make the decision beforehand to not work on vacation. A true vacation is time away from life at home, and that means work.

Your vacation plans are beginning to materialize: You have set your budget, begun researching your destination, and have prepared for how to get from here to there. In the next chapter, you will learn more about why so many people are experiencing multigenerational vacations. So before you set your vacation plans in stone, consider bringing along some family members.

. THREE .

Have Family, Will Travel

The Lure of Multigenerational Travel

*O*n a recent Disney cruise through the Caribbean with my family, my son, Charlie, made pals with a boy his age who introduced himself as Ray Ray. The two hit it off, enjoying themselves on the rock-climbing wall that scaled the third tier of the boat, at the billiard tables, and at the indoor swimming pool (you will learn much more about the various types of cruises in Chapter 8. On day three of their hanging out together, Charlie learned some interesting things about his newfound friend: 1) Ray Ray was born in Russia; 2) "Ray Ray" wasn't his real name but a nickname; his given name was Vladimir; 3) he had two fathers; and 4) he was traveling with one of his grandmothers. Charlie didn't bat an eye, but I found myself thinking about how the concept and reality of family is changing and expanding and that this is nowhere more evident than how families decide to vacation.

According to the Travel Association of America (TAA), one in three vacations taken by families includes at least one grandparent, and TAA cites several reasons for this trend. One of them is economic. With the cost of living continually going up, pooling resources makes taking that otherwise impossible dream vacation possible. Another key reason is that today many extended families live far apart, and taking a vacation together gives Grandma and Grandpa a chance to spend some quality time not only with their grandkids but with their own kids, as well. Last, as in the case with Ray Ray (aka Vladimir), extended family members might have more time for vacation. Ray Ray's two dads were unable to take vacation at the same time as he, so rather than have her grandson stay home for his break, his grandmother decided to take him on a Disney cruise.

As our lives continue to become busier and more complicated, and extended families continue to be spread far apart, multigenerational travel is fast becoming a practical and enjoyable way for families to stay connected and enjoy one another's company.

Why Travel with Your Parents and In-laws

While it's true that some people reel at the thought of taking a vacation with their in-laws or even their own parents, there are a lot of pluses to such a situation. Though you aren't bringing them as babysitters, having Grandma and Grandpa around can make carving out your alone time with your significant other a whole lot easier. As one parent, Mary, said of her last vacation, "We rented a beach house on the South Carolina coast. Because my parents were coming we got a bigger house with a pool and outdoor Jacuzzi—something my husband and I could not afford on our own—and also had an opportunity to have not one but two romantic dinners without the kids! My parents were delighted to hang out with our teenage sons—they had a ball going to the nearby miniature golf park!"

Another parent shared this: "At first I was reluctant to invite my mother-in-law along for our ski vacation. I mean, she doesn't ski—what was she going to do all day? But my kids loved having her around, and I realized that since she lives on the other coast, they don't get to just hang out together very often."

It used to be fairly commonplace for grandparents (and extended family members) to be involved in the daily lives of their adult children and grandchildren, watching them grow, spending time on weekends, babysitting, and so on. But as Americans continue to move away from their hometowns, establishing their adult lives far away from where they were raised, it's more the exception than the rule that grandparents and grandchildren live in the same town. As Margaret explained, "As a kid growing up I spent my entire summer vacation at the beach, and so did all my cousins, aunts and uncles, great-aunts and great-uncles, and grandparents. We were an enormous extended family. But all that's changed. Now the way I stay in touch is to plan trips with different members of my family. Last winter, I planned a vacation with my uncle. We all met in Florida for Easter—and it was great. Next year, we're going to try Aruba!"

Avoiding Potential Conflicts

Many people dread family reunions at the old homestead: Past tensions have a way of springing up when adults are in their childhood setting. As one man explained, "Last Thanksgiving was a disaster. We all went home to my parents' in Ohio. They live in the same house where my three brothers and I were raised. By the end of the evening, no one was talking because we had all begun to argue about the stupidest things." What had been the source of tension? His mother had asked the brothers to clean up!

One benefit of having an extended family travel to a destination away from home is that the vacation spot—whether hotel, condo, or cruise ship—provides neutral ground for families to spend time with one another. Some families fear traveling together, dreading old tensions and conflicts that could ruin their precious vacation time. But there are some ways to anticipate and thereby avoid such trouble.

If your extended family gathers on neutral territory, there is much less of a chance for family conflict, but this doesn't mean that all family squabbles are avoidable. One client told me of a disastrous ski trip in which four different families rented a lodgelike house at a ski resort at Mad River Glen in Maine. "Aunt Sue" had made the arrangements and, a bit overzealous in her role as hausfrau, had posted a bulletin board of everyone's daily chores. Although such a large group does need a lead person to provide some sort of organization, Aunt Sue's strident tone (she checked up on all chores) ended up alienating everyone—from her and from one another. By the end of the week, the house was filled with tension and everyone was having a miserable time.

So though I encourage you to have some rules, I also think it's important that the tone in which these rules are established and delivered needs to be one of fairness and a sense of play. After all, you're on vacation! Is there someone in the family who likes to do research about the area your family is planning on visiting? Another person who is good at numbers and might enjoy organizing how to pay the bills? Is another family member good at arranging airport pickups and other travel arrangements? It's a good idea to give people certain jobs so that everyone stays involved but has his or her own role to play.

Selecting a Destination

Multigenerational travel can work—and work well—but it necessitates planning and flexibility. In the last chapter I advised that when planning a family vacation you should keep the prime decision-making between just you and your partner and include your children in the process. But this is not true when you're planning an extended family vacation; this time, you'll want input from everyone. You will also want to start planning well in advance, at least six months and up to a year.

As you begin the process of deciding where to go and managing the planning stage of a multigenerational trip, you want to take the following steps:

- Know your audience. Who is involved? What are their ages? Does anyone have specific health restrictions?

- Poll your group for their general goals for the vacation. Do they want to spend time with the family, hanging out? Does most of the group want to participate in active sports and other activities? Are some of the older folks interested in touring and sightseeing? Are there young family members who require child care? Once you know exactly whom your group consists of, you can begin to make specific recommendations for destinations.

- Determine everyone's budget level. This is obvious, but many families have different ideas of what's expensive, moderate, and cheap. Make sure you all know what each family wants to spend.

- Select and then suggest a small handful of places and encourage everyone to do their own hands-on research. Have individual families do an Internet search (many resorts have virtual tours), or ask the resorts to mail brochures to family members.

- Decide on a place based on the input gathered from all family members, and then send out information about activities, accommodations, dining, and other pertinent details so that everyone is armed with the necessary information.

• Remember, as you choose your destination, be honest about what
kind of experience you want from the vacation. If you love the
beach and sun, then don't make one of your choices a vacation
destination with a lot of snow; you may resent it later when your
siblings select it from your choice of options. And make sure you
remind all the other family members to be equally honest. If conflicts arise and two (or more) parties cannot come to an agree-
ment, suggest one or two options as a compromise. Some
families do a blind vote in such cases, with no one revealing
which destination they chose but everyone agreeing in advance
to accept the majority choice.

But let's back up. Maybe like so many others, you're at a loss as to
where to even start to research multigenerational vacations—it can
feel overwhelming! No worries. A number of companies can help you
plan a multigenerational trip. These companies organize the complete
trip for families, including travel arrangements, activities, meal plans,
and excursions. The price of this level of organizing and planning is
built in to the per-person cost of the trip, which can be a bit steep, but
it can be worth the expense to have a non–family member in charge.
Three organizations stand out from the crowd.

• ***Grand Travel (www.grandtrvl.com)*** specializes in first-class
trips around the United States, Europe, and Africa for grandparents
and their grandchildren, though the adult need not be a biological
grandparent. Recent trips have taken groups to Alaska and Washington, D.C., through the American Southwest, as well as to a special dinosaur expedition in Colorado's red-rock country. Outside of the
United States, trips have been organized to London and Paris, Scot-
land, Italy, Australia, and China. Grand Travel's mission is to foster the
special mentor relationship and bond between the older generation

and their grandkids so that both can grow. By offering en route activities, traditional and local meals, and counseling, this organization has thought of every need.

• ***Generational Touring Company (www.generationstouringcompany.com)*** is a family-owned organization that offers tours for multigenerational family groups to exciting destinations around the globe. It prides itself on being able to offer intimate bonding experiences while at the same encouraging everyone to have fun in an interesting new culture. Recent trips have taken families to the Galápagos Islands, Costa Rica, and Mexico. Another exciting adventure took families on a tour of historic baseball parks, where they watched American League rivals in action and toured Boston, New York City, and Cooperstown, including the Baseball Hall of Fame.

• ***Disney (www.magicalgatherings.com)*** understands families and encourages large groups of family members to come and enjoy its splendors through its Magical Gatherings program. This free service is offered by specialists who will plan entire Disney vacations for large groups. Disney sets up a Web site for your family so that all family members can give their input about where they want to visit, what types of food they like, what their individual budgets are, and how much time they would like to spend as a group. Once one family member contacts the Magical Gatherings people at Disney World, they do the rest! They send out e-mails requesting information and organize itineraries based on individual and group interests, and they even will plan dinner parties! Disney also provides an incentive for you to use their service by offering added items such as a free nighttime safari dinner cruise in the Wild Kingdom or a scheduled photo op in front of the castle at the Magic Kingdom. Need I say more? If Disney World is your destination, you are off to a great start!

Another great option for multigenerational travel is a cruise, which offers something for everyone, of every age and every taste. As you will see in Chapter 8, cruises vary in style, price, and length. Begin by looking into what the major cruise lines offer. A good one to check out is Norwegian Cruise Lines (www.ncl.com), which, unlike most cruise ships, doesn't require formal attire in the majority of its restaurants. Another good choice is Royal Caribbean Cruise Lines (www.rccl.com), which offers everything from rock climbing for the kids to spa services for the adults. Last but not least is Disney Cruise Line (www.disneycruise.com), which also offers a myriad of wonderful activities for everyone.

Accommodations That Make Sense

When you're planning a trip for a group of various ages, it's important to choose lodging where everyone can be comfortable. While some grandparents may not mind sleeping on a pullout sofa in the middle of a condo, many need more privacy, including a private bathroom. Finding the best place to stay should include a detailed inventory of what types of sleeping arrangements are available.

As a lot of places get hip to multigenerational travel, many resorts and hotels are offering great options. For example, the Marriott Vacation Club (www.marriott.com) offers two-bedroom villas with fully stocked kitchens where you can all be together but still have your privacy, all the while keeping the price fairly reasonable. Many families request and rely on the amenity of a full kitchen—to give kids an easy breakfast in the morning, let Grandma make her eleven a.m. cup of tea, and give Grandpa his midnight fix of huevos rancheros. Plus, not only is preparing your own meals a great way to save money, but sharing a home-cooked meal is a simple way to spend valuable family time together.

Another travel company that offers good sleeping options is the RCI Holiday Network, which offers a wide selection of vacation condominiums and single-family homes for rent in the United States, Canada, Mexico, and the Caribbean. Just go to www.rcihn.com or call 1-866-844-2018. And last, you can check out www.craigslist.com, a multidimensional Web site that posts information directly between renters and people looking to rent. Here you can actually swap your home in Virginia for someone else's villa in Colorado—the catch is that this is done based on trust between people, so there is no guarantee of anything. Still, I have heard of some people who have had nice experiences using this Internet source.

Plan Your Itinerary

Once you've decided on your destination, whether it's Disney World or the Norwegian Cruise Line, then it's time to start planning the vacation itself—what you'll do day to day. When you're planning, it's important to keep in mind everyone's schedules. Maybe your parents sleep in later than you and the kids or your toddler needs to take a nap every afternoon promptly at two p.m. For this reason, it's important to get input from everyone, but without letting it get out of control! As I have suggested, delegate roles for organizing and researching information about your destination, making one or two people in charge of gathering information about activities, tours, and other recreation. Again, some multigenerational planners, including Disney, have a Web-based planner that allows you to have chat groups about your itinerary, send out invitations, and create a day-to-day calendar—this is a great, democratic way to give everyone a voice in the plans and also helps keep all the responsibility from falling on your shoulders! On the other hand, if you are planning your own multigenerational trip and your kids are techno savvy, give them the project of setting up a Web site for all group members to visit as the plans are being made and developed. It's a great way to keep touching base with everyone and help to build the excitement for the trip!

One thing to keep in mind when you're planning your daily schedule is that you don't have to spend every moment together. Some families, like the Thorntons of Santa Fe, New Mexico, decided that they would go their separate ways during the day and meet up in the evening, for dinner. Others, like the Harveys, chose to spend some days together and others apart. They weren't afraid to mix and match family members: Some days, for example, the children spent the whole day with their grandparents, leaving Mom and Dad alone to spend some quality time together. Other days, the kids were with Mom and Dad, and Grandpa and Grandma got to enjoy a peaceful day of reading at the condo and resting.

If the kids are old enough, particularly if you're on a cruise, where the likelihood of their getting into trouble is minimal, some days or parts of days you can let them go off on their own—there are plenty of organized, chaperoned activities on board (or at a resort) to keep them happily occupied.

Reunions and Other Family Gatherings

Although any multigenerational trip has some feel of a family reunion, honest-to-God family reunions usually mean a much larger group of more than one family. Organizing for such a trip can be quite overwhelming. Edith Wagner, editor of *Reunions* magazine, shared her advice for planning a family reunion.

Start early. Develop a plan that takes all interests, ages, incomes, and abilities into account. What does your family like to do? Locating a site may be the single hardest decision facing the family reunion organizer looking for something bigger than her backyard. Some choose to make reunions into family vacations, selecting an exotic locale like a dude ranch, resort, ski lodge, houseboat, or cruise ship. Other alternatives are resident camps, villas, or condos that can be leased for a week. For a rustic camping adventure, try a national or state park with cabins or camping facilities. A more ambitious plan is an international reunion, which can allow everyone to explore family history and has the added bonus of bringing together relatives from different countries. Another way to stimulate interest in family roots is to plan a reunion at an original family homesite or farm.

Ask for reunion services from convention and visitors' bureaus in areas that interest you, including your own area, if the reunion is coming to you. Many hotels eagerly court reunion groups with designated reunion sales staff. Check Reunion Resources at www.reunionsmag.com, *Reunions* magazine's list of reunion-friendly places. Then explore the Web site for more reunion planning ideas and complete the survey for a free sample of the magazine.

Staying at Someone's Home

Regardless of whether your family is gathering for a reunion or simply making a family visit, staying at a family member's home requires a certain delicacy. Consider these tips:

- Surrender to the house rules. When visiting the in-laws or other family members, warn your children to respect how the family lives. You need to both prep them so they know what to expect and quietly remind them once you arrive. For instance, if you know that Aunt Carol is a real neatnik, then make sure your kids pay extra attention to cleaning up after themselves. If Uncle Charlie and Aunt Sheila forbid eating in front of the television, which you allow at your house, then respect the house rule and eat at the kitchen table.

- Be more considerate than usual. This tip applies as much to us adults as it does to kids. If you like starting your day with a long shower, you may have to forgo it while staying at Grandma's. Do you want to be blamed for the lack of hot water?

- Respect everyone's possessions. If your kids are young, make sure they understand that their cousins' or friends' toys are not their own. When visiting the home of friends, prepare your kids to respect the toys of the other kids.

- Announce any illness. If your kids are sick, you should warn the other families beforehand. You may consider staying in separate accommodations until no one is contagious.

- Parent your way. Don't be afraid to handle your kids' meltdowns in the way you do at home. However, you might consider trying to establish a bit of privacy first so the group does not have to witness the scene.

- Consider staying elsewhere. Instead of cramming into Grandma's house, stay at a nearby hotel or inn. If you think your family really will have a difficult time adapting to a family member's house rules, then you might be better off staying elsewhere. A little distance could help maintain good relationships.

- Stay neat and tidy. This is another rule that applies to kids and adults. Don't leave your clothes strewn about someone's house, and help keep the kitchen clean by bringing your plates to the sink or putting them in the dishwasher. Don't assume you can do laundry.

- If you don't drive your own car, you might consider renting one so you don't have to rely on borrowing someone else's. You are then more free to do your own thing and your host family doesn't have to drive you everywhere you want to go.

• *Golden Moment Rule #3* •

Take a Deep Breath!

When I was helping my then four-year-old daughter Gabby to manage her feelings instead of pitching a temper tantrum or breaking into cries of anguish whenever things didn't go her way, I used to say, "Okay, Gabby, now take a deep breath." Slowly but surely she learned how to have a feeling before she reacted all over the place. I'm convinced that if you learn this lesson about feelings early in life, managing your emotions later in life becomes a lot easier. That's why I offer this advice: When we are around our families, we all tend to regress just a wee bit. It's easy to start acting like ten when we're forty, eight when we're fifty, and six when we're close to eighty. You can't make all familial issues disappear during a multigenerational vacation, but you can take a deep breath instead of reacting—or overreacting—to things people say or do. As the Jamaicans say, Peace, mon, peace.

Checklist for Planning a Multigenerational Vacation

- ❑ Identify who is in your group.
- ❑ Think about the age ranges. Does anyone have any special health or medical needs?
- ❑ Talk about what everyone is interested in doing. Have you polled the group for their activities, entertainment, dining, and other recreation interests?
- ❑ Evaluate everyone's budget.
- ❑ Based on the group's interests, budgets, and needs, select two to three options for a vacation and survey the group for everyone's choice.

❏ Select one destination and appoint one person to gather information and send it to each group member.

❏ Arrange loose schedules or itineraries for the trip.

One final thing to keep in mind when you're planning your multigenerational vacation: Stuff happens, so stay flexible. Again, if you
arm yourself with information, you can have interesting options at your
fingertips for backup plans for your daily itinerary. But the key to
adapting and adjusting to snafus such as museum closings, inclement
weather, or an illness in the family is to be open to possible changes
and to remember that the real reason for your trip is to be with one another. More people means more agendas. Multigenerational travel requires more patience with fewer expectations and that everyone be
accommodating of the needs and wants of others. You may want to
save your dream trip for another time, when you can have more say
and control. For a multigenerational trip, it's best to go with the flow
and keep the peace.

. FOUR .

Shh! Don't Tell the Kids They're Learning

Educational Experiences on Vacation

Y*ou might* think that giving your children an educational experience while on vacation will only elicit cries of anguish and boredom. This doesn't have to be the case.

I always think of one of my favorite stories, about a vacation the Elias family took to New York. Sarah, a mother of three girls—then ages eight, ten, and twelve—took her family to see the Museum of Natural History. She figured the girls would get bored after an hour or so, but she was shocked to discover that her kids couldn't get enough of the dinosaurs and then were absolutely captivated by the planetarium. As they stood gazing upward at the giants of yesteryear and contemplating the galaxies, Sarah and her husband had one of their own magical moments in which they realized how fortunate they were to be able to enjoy themselves so completely.

Creating an Educational Element

Including an educational element in your family vacation is not as difficult or boring as you (or your kids) may think. Almost all vacations are educational to some degree—you learn about a new place, try a new kind of food, experience the world from a different vantage point. A trip to Legoland can be educational, and so can a dolphin encounter. Any time a child immerses himself in a new experience, he stretches his mind. So how do you go about making sure you include one in your vacation? Consider this quick list:

- Visit a historical site in the area.
- Attend a cultural event or festival.
- Dine in an ethnic restaurant.
- Shop in an ethnic neighborhood—a number of cities have great Chinatowns.
- Go to an art museum.
- Visit a science museum.
- Commune with nature and its flora or fauna.

What follows is a list of ideas to get you started. You wouldn't plan a whole trip around one of these visits, but if you are in the area, you might want to include it on your itinerary.

Museums Can Be Mystical

Wonderful children's museums are popping up all over the country. Almost every city has at least one museum in which children can learn and have fun both interactively and through observation. Most children's museums also offer exhibits and activities for various age groups. Some good ones include the following:

Northeast

• **The Eric Carle Museum of Picture Book Art in Amherst, Massachusetts** offers plenty of interactive learning for your children to participate in. Mr. Carle, the author-illustrator of wonderful books such as *The Hungry Caterpillar,* is often in the museum to read one of his children's books aloud. The library offers story hour, and the art studio encourages children to sit down and get creative. Visit www.picturebookart.com.

• **The Academy of Natural Sciences in Philadelphia** is a museum, library, and discovery center all in one. Kids can meet and talk to different scientists and learn about what they do, immerse themselves in ways to protect the environment, and spend the night with dinosaurs! This is a must-see if you head to Philadelphia. For more information, contact www.acnatsci.org.

• **The American Museum of Natural History in New York City** is not to be missed. The museum is home to the world-famous Hayden Planetarium in the Rose Center for Earth and Space, where kids can be transported to the beginning of time and space, and the Milstein Hall of Ocean Life, with a full-immersion marine environment. The museum also offers annual events, such as the Butterfly Conservatory. For more information, contact www.amnh.org.

South

• **The Alexandria Museum of Art in Alexandria, Louisiana,** is a treat for both you and the kids. While you're touring its interesting exhibit of works by top artists from Louisiana, the kids can play in its interactive art and multimedia gallery. See www.themuseum.org.

• ***Atlanta's Imagine It! Children's Museum*** offers a cornucopia of children's activities and learning experiences, including interactive programs in which kids can dance and play music and visit outer space, as well as hands-on exhibits about different foods and tools. For more information, contact www.imagineit-cma.org.

Southwest

• ***The Arizona Museum for Youth in Mesa, Arizona,*** features activities and games that introduce children to basic artistic principles. Visit www.ci.mesa.az.us/amfy.

Midwest

• ***The Betty Brinn Children's Museum in Milwaukee, Wisconsin,*** gears great art exhibits for children up to ten years old. See www.bbcmkids.org.

• ***The Children's Museum of Kansas City, Kansas,*** is a thoughtful, well-integrated learning center for kids. Children can participate in a theater program, experience a ride in an ambulance, and explore life under the city streets. For more information, contact www.kidmuzm.org.

• ***The Buffalo Bill Historical Center in Cody, Wyoming,*** is one of the best western museums in the country and is only fifty-two miles away from Yellowstone National Park—so maybe you could include this in between all that hiking!

West Coast

• **A. C. Gilbert's Discovery Village in Salem, Oregon,** is famous for its hands-on exhibits for children, such as shadow boxing, optical illusions, and bubbles! See www.acgilbert.org.

• **The Bay Area Discovery Museum,** just under the North Tower of the Golden Gate Bridge in Sausalito, California, offers numerous fun, interactive scientific exhibits for kids. Contact www.baykidsmuseum.org for more information.

• **The Exploratorium in San Francisco** is housed within the walls of San Francisco's Palace of Fine Arts. The Exploratorium is a collage of hundreds of science, art, and human perception exhibits. For more information, contact www.exploratorium.edu.

• **ZEUM,** also in San Francisco, has amazing interactive technical games for young kids as well as teens. For more information, visit www.zeum.org.

Don't discount art museums that are not specifically geared toward young people, either. Indeed, traditional art museums are great sources of educational pleasures, and many museums are becoming quite crafty about attracting young people with exhibits meant to engage their imaginations, passions, and curiosity. Most cities have at least one major art museum, and in Chapter 11, I mention many wonderful art museums that children will enjoy.

Here is a short list of fascinating art museums across the country:

• Museum of Fine Arts in Boston
• Isabella Stewart Gardner Museum in Boston
• Philadelphia Museum of Art

- Barnes Museum in Philadelphia
- De Menil Museum in Houston
- Getty Museum in Los Angeles
- Metropolitan Museum of Art in New York City
- Museum of Modern Art in New York City
- Smithsonian Museums in Washington, D.C., and other cities

When you tackle museums—big or small—with kids, it's important not to overdo it. Select one or two exhibits to meander around. Then take a rest. Go outside if weather permits. Get something to eat or drink. Museums are mentally taxing to adults—just imagine the sensory overload they can deliver to children!

A SPECIAL MUSEUM

*T*he Holocaust Museum in Washington, D.C., contains a separate wing and group of exhibits especially geared to children. With its softened tone and information and installations geared toward younger minds, this section is truly remarkable in its ability to capture one of the world's most horrible tragedies. Because of the seriousness of the subject matter and graphic material, it may not be suitable to all children, especially very young ones. You know best.

Children's Theater

Most children enjoy going to live performances of plays and musicals, and many cities offer well-produced productions at established children's theaters. Some theaters geared to children present original theatrical productions, and others present adult plays adapted for children. Your children will have a ball at these marvelous children's theaters:

• *The Lexington Children's Theater of Lexington, Kentucky,* was founded in 1938 and has been putting on live performances for children ever since. A recent production was *Miss Nelson Is Missing,* an adaptation of a children's book. (www.lctonstage.org)

• *Birmingham Children's Theatre,* founded in 1947 by the Junior League of Birmingham, Alabama, has recently put such classics as *The Little Red Hen, The Frog Prince,* and *The Prince and the Pauper,* among many others. (www.bct123.org)

• *The Broadway Palm West Children's Theatre,* located outside of Phoenix, Arizona, combines lunch and a play in the price of admission. Recent productions include *Sleeping Beauty, Pinocchio,* and *Jack and the Beanstalk.* (www.broadwaypalmwest.com)

• *Children's Musical Theater in San Jose, California,* puts on first-rate productions of musicals such as *Chess* and *Seussical.* (www.cmtsj.org)

You can access information about children's theater near your destination through two sources, the Artslynx International (www.artslynx.org) and the Children's Resource page developed by the theater faculty at Northwestern University (www.faculty-web.at.northwestern.edu/theater).

Zoomania

Many children and adults love animals, and there are several ways to combine the pleasures of observing animals and learning about wildlife. Of course, most cities have a local zoo. One of my favorites is the Zoo at Naples (formerly known as Jungle Larry's African Safari Park Caribbean Gardens) in Naples, Florida, which is geared toward education and conservation and includes a solar-powered audio tour with musical jingles for kids. Another one of my favorites is the Cincinnati Zoo & Botanical Garden, which, besides being one of the oldest zoos in the country, is home to two Sumatran (woolly) rhinoceroses—mother and child—quite a remarkable occurrence. As the museum's logo states, "You might travel the world and see many sights, many places, many creatures. But only in Cincinnati or in the impenetrable forests of South Asia will you see the unique and endearing sight of a mother Sumatran rhino and her calf." Like museums, zoos offer great classes, tours, and other interactive exhibits for kids. When you are planning your visit to a particular city, contact the zoo to see what special events are taking place while you're there.

Here are some more great zoos in our country to visit!

Northeast

• **The Bronx Zoo, Bronx, New York**—Go face-to-face with western lowland gorillas in the famous Congo Gorilla Forest, see snow leopards in the Himalayan Highlands Habitat, or experience almost an acre of an indoor Asian rain forest. (www.bronxzoo.com)

• **Smithsonian National Zoological Park, Washington, D.C.**—Visit baby cheetahs in the African savannah, as well as Asian elephants, tigers, pandas, and more in this enormous national zoo. (www.nationalzoo.si.edu)

South and Southwest

• **The Memphis Zoo**—This is one of only eleven zoos in the country where visitors can view pandas. They also offer overnight zoo experiences for children and their parents. (www.memphiszoo.org)

• *Fort Worth Zoo, Fort Worth, Texas*—This special place offers a five-day resident Career Camp for high schoolers, as well as overnight safaris and Parrot Paradise, a tremendous bird exhibit. (www.fortworth-zoo.org)

• *Henry Doorly's Zoo, Omaha, Nebraska*—In the Hubbard Gorilla Valley, gorillas roam free on two acres. (www.omahazoo.com)

Midwest

• *The Detroit Zoological Park & Belle Isle Zoo & Aquarium*—This zoo offers a summer safari and kingdom of the Hunter, a weeklong adventure for kids, as well as daylong adventures that include Butterfly Capers, Animal Enrichment, and Dino Digs. (www.detroitzoo.org)

• *Indianapolis Zoo, Indianapolis, Indiana*—This zoo is home to the nation's first totally submerged underwater dolphin viewing experience. (www.indyzoo.org)

• *St. Louis Zoo, St. Louis, Missouri*—This zoo hosts the Fragile Forest, a new outdoor habitat for orangutans and chimpanzees, and offers great programs throughout summer for families and kids, including sleepovers and night hikes. (www.stlzoo.org)

West

• *Oregon Zoo, Portland, Oregon*—This zoo is part of the California Condor Recovery Program and offers much more, including a Bear Family Encounter. (www.oregonzoo.com)

• *San Diego Zoo, San Diego, California*—Its Lion Camp and Monkey Trails, the country's largest and most elaborate habitat, and Panda Park are world famous. (www.sandiegozoo.org)

Wild, Wild Life

If your kids are animal lovers, there are many ways to let them experience wildlife—from visiting a working farm, to observing wildlife while on a cruise excursion, to staying at a dude ranch or becoming part of a "zoo crew." If you are heading to Florida, the Caribbean, or Mexico, you might also want to look into intimate encounters with sea life, including dolphins, manatees, and even whales. The following are few special places for you to consider:

• *Cedar Creek at Spruce Hill B&B, Spruce Creek, Pennsylvania*—This working farm with cattle, chickens, honeybees, and rabbits invites families to spend fun weekends gathering eggs, playing with the bunnies, or even suiting up to visit the hives. Your family can investigate the nearby caves or go berry picking. Fishing and swimming are also available.

• *Craig Ranch, Limon, Colorado*—At this 15,000-acre working cattle ranch eighty miles east of Denver, children can enjoy a firsthand view of gathering and branding cattle. You can try your hand at spinning wool and ride with ranch hands to participate in roundups.

• *Busch Gardens in Tampa Bay, Florida*—Busch Gardens Tampa Bay offers a one-day program that allows kids to shadow zookeepers as they perform their duties from sunup to sunset. Kids will feed, groom, and care for animals on the Serengeti Desert area alongside trained professionals. During the day, they will enjoy lunch at the Gardens' upscale restaurant and observe the animals from their seats. This program has limited space so that you can have a hands-on, intimate experience. (www.buschgardens.com)

• *Sea World*—Each of the three Sea World locations offers something special. Besides shows, rides, and attractions, each Sea World features special events in its parks. Visitors to Sea World San Diego can participate in the Trainer for a Day program. Participants work alongside real animal trainers, perfecting behaviors and caring for the animals. You can also get wet and educated in a dolphin interaction program. The San Antonio park offers a selection of up-close encounters with marine life. Beluga whales, sea lions, and even sharks are a part of their educational hands-on programs. Guided, behind-the-scenes tours and sleepovers in the park are available, too. In Orlando, you can don a wetsuit and swim with more than fifty sharks. You can watch and learn as sharks glide by you in the water. The Polar Expedition allows guests to explore backstage at the Wild Arctic exhibit and learn all about penguins. (www.seaworld.com)

Historical Sites

Children can learn so much from visiting the many historic sites around our country. One woman, Charlotte, recently told me of her trip with her fourteen-year-old son, in which they visited all the major Civil War battleground sites, including Gettysburg, Savannah, and Atlanta. As she recounted to me, "At times it was creepy. You could really feel the depth of history beneath your feet." Several organizations specialize in guided tours of the Civil War sites, including Civil War Tours at www.civilwartours.org.

Another great spot for exploring historical landmarks is in and around the city of Boston. You can take kids to the site of the Boston Tea Party, Paul Revere's home, or the battlefield of the Minute Men in Lexington, just outside the city. The Boston Preservation Alliance has a great Web site at www.bostonpreservation.org.

As our nation's capital, Washington, D.C., is home to a number of historical events, monuments, and testaments to our country's interesting and challenging history. The Capitol Hill and National Mall areas contain many of the most important sites, including the White House, the Capitol, the Library of Congress, and the Supreme Court. On the National Mall, you will find the Smithsonian Institution, which contains several museums, and many memorials, including the Washington Monument, the Lincoln Memorial, and the Vietnam Veterans Memorial.

Historical landmarks exist in every part of the country, so either choose by destination or choose by historical point of interest. Take a look at Chapter 11 for more information on historical sites within cities across the United States.

Learn Something New

Vacations provide great opportunities to learn a new hobby. It's always good—and fun—to stimulate the old brain and other parts of your body you haven't used in a while. For example, Cynthia always talked about how she wished she could paint. Finally, when she, her husband, and children went on vacation in Hawaii, she took a weeklong painting class consisting of five ninety-minute sessions. When she got home, she found room in her already packed schedule to continue her art class!

Another woman, Colleen, said one of her most memorable trips was when she and her daughter went to surf camp together in Baja California. Before, she did not imagine that she would enjoy surfing and couldn't see herself actually getting up on the surfboard. But she did!

Or what about that Spanish you've been dying to improve? Well, consider a vacation in San Antonio—what better place to practice your Spanish in a mini language class? It'll get your juices flowing, and you just might keep it up when you go home.

That little course you've been thinking about may turn out to be the best thing you ever did. One family decided to take bridge lessons while on a cruise. The Tremblys—mother, father, and two daughters, ages ten and twelve—had a blast learning this intricate card game.

Taking a class is a great way to learn a new skill and have some fun. A woman named Sandra took a parasailing class during her vacation in sunny Cabo San Lucas that changed her life. Why? Before Sandra took the class she had a chronic fear of taking risks. Even going on vacation felt like a bit of a risk for her because she didn't like to go far from home. So when the concierge at her hotel suggested she take parasailing lessons, she just laughed. But her husband kept talking about it all week, and on the second to last day of the vacation, feeling relaxed and rejuvenated from all the fun in the sun, she surprised him and her two kids by taking the lesson. Sandra says that day changed her life in the most beautiful, bountiful way.

I'm not promising that your life is going to do a one-eighty like Sandra's, but you may be pleasantly surprised at how much a person can learn at forty, fifty, sixty, and even on into her seventies and eighties.

Once in a Lifetime Educational Experience:

Williamsburg, Virginia

One of the best ways for children to learn about their country's history is through immersion, and Colonial Williamsburg in Virginia offers a unique opportunity. This historic town is a virtual living museum where you and your family can fully experience what it was like to live in eighteenth-century colonial America. Children can watch actors dressed up in eighteenth-century clothes, telling the stories and acting out the lives of your average blacksmith, indentured servant, slave, and other people who might have lived in this town a few centuries ago.

Like their eighteenth-century counterparts, kids can dress up, learn to sew, dance, play, and do daily chores. They can sample and learn to prepare dishes that were common at this time, including gazpacho, gingerbread, Dutch apple dumplings, and shepherd's pie. The museum offers an extensive interactive media system, enabling children to explore life in Colonial Williamsburg on their own. And the shopping is great! The small shops mirror the products used at the time, with candles and sealing wax, three-cornered hats, and eighteenth-century remedies and medicinal herbs available for purchase.

Accommodations are varied and plentiful. You can stay at one of several colonial-style inns or bed-and-breakfasts or at one of twenty-eight colonial-style houses in the historic area. Your family can spend one, two, or three days in this remarkable town, making it a destination all its own.

If you want a break from colonial America, you and the kids can enjoy yourselves at nearby Busch Gardens, with its theme park and Kingsmill Spa & Resort, which has a kids' camp, three golf courses, and spa services.

For further information about planning a trip to Williamsburg, contact www.history.org.

Checklist for Adding an Educational Experience

- ❏ Research the museums in the area you are planning to visit.
- ❏ Determine whether the city you are visiting has a children's museum.
- ❏ Inquire whether the children's museum offers any hands-on learning experiences for kids.
- ❏ Check out the zoos in the area and inquire about special events.
- ❏ See if there are any festivals occurring while you're in a particular city or town.
- ❏ Consider a trip to a nearby city and have an adventure!

Are you almost ready to choose a destination? Do you imagine yourself on a beach with a good book, palm trees waving peacefully in the background? Or do you want to take your kids on their first winter va-

· PART TWO ·

Destinations

• *Golden Moment Rule #4* •

Give Your Kids Your Presence

*T*he best way our children learn—that is, absorb and retain information—is by feeling connected and grounded. Connected and grounded to *us*. Life outside of vacation is very hectic and busy, and it's often quite a challenge to give our kids the focus and attention they need. Vacation is the perfect time to make a conscious effort to offer them this gift.

---

cation and maybe even hit the slopes? Perhaps you want to experience a cruise for the first time? Whatever your travel mood, you will find the perfect destination for you and your family in Part 2.

. FIVE .

Beach Vacations and Other Warm-Weather Trips

*T*he beach is one of many people's favorite places to visit. The ocean is calming, the sea air both invigorating and soothing, and the beach—any time of year—can be relaxing for both adults and children. As one woman said, "A day at the beach is the perfect way for everyone to get a great night's sleep!" This mix of enjoyment and relaxation is what make beach vacations so terrific for families. And once you decide on where you want to go, beach vacations don't require that much planning. All you have to do is get there!

When I was a little girl, my parents used to load us up in the car every summer and we would drive from Phoenix to San Diego. We rented a beach house for two weeks, and all we did was spend time at the beach. We collected sand crabs and rode the waves and slept really well. It was never overplanned or overscheduled, and it was always a great vacation.

Many families enjoy their vacations at the beach, whether they wait for summer when the kids are out of school or decide to find a warm oceanside spot during winter. With the United States surrounded by water, there is no shortage of options for families who like to take trips to the seashore. From New England's ragged and varied coastline, to the more mellow tidal shores of the mid-Atlantic states, to Florida's legendary eastern coast and around its tip to the quiet luxury of its Gulf coast, to the entrancing Gulf coast beaches of other states, including Alabama, Louisiana, and Texas, to all of California, Oregon, and Washington, the beach of your dreams awaits you. Many people who grew up going to lakes consider the shores of the Great Lakes beaches indeed.

Though there is not space enough to describe the many beaches this country has to offer, I will highlight a handful of my favorites, as well as offer you tips on how best to enjoy a vacation by the shore. You will also find beach destinations in the Caribbean and Mexico described in Chapter 7 on all-inclusive resorts, as well as some mentioned in Chapter 8 on cruises, which often port in exquisite beach towns. Beautiful beaches also exist outside our shores, including some of the finest in Europe, Southeast Asia, and Australia. Suffice it to say that going beyond the shores of North America would fill the pages of another book!

Beachy Keen

If your family is anything like mine, you and your kids know that there's no better place to unwind or be active than at the beach. But before deciding where you want to go to spend your beach vacation, consider the following.

What time of year are you planning to travel? Of course, you may associate beach vacations primarily with summers by the seashore. And though summer is an ideal time to enjoy the sun, surf, and sand, families can enjoy trips to some beach areas during the off-season. When you do travel outside the heavy-traffic months of June, July, and August, you might find some money-saving options!

Where do you want to stay? Many families prefer to rent condominiums or houses on or near the beach, and most beach areas offer plenty of local rentals for both short term (one- or two-week stays) or long term (a month or two). It's true that some beach destinations are more naturally suited to a weekend visit and others attract families wanting to stay for longer stretches of time. Once you decide on your destination, you can look into local area condo or house rentals, as well as resorts, hotels, motels, camping, and RVing options.

Beaches can be windy; beaches can be rainy. To be weather-prepared for a vacation at the seashore, I always slip in a sweatshirt and light rain jacket for kids. For myself, I throw in a couple of long-sleeve T-shirts, a beach cover-up, and a pair of long pants, which are handy both for cooler weather and to minimize sun exposure. I prefer wearing light terry-cloth or linenlike drawstring pants that can withstand being rolled into a beach bag or backpack.

Although we like to think of a beach vacation as one long, relaxing day at the beach, you and your kids will probably tire of going to the beach every single day of your vacation. With that in mind, consider other entertainment options in the area.

Beach regions often offer a great range of activities, including water sports such as sea kayaking and canoeing, sailing, Jet Skiing, tennis and golf, horseback riding, and, of course, shopping—every mother's favorite sport. Some beach areas also offer great fishing, marine life experiences, and festivals, especially during the summer months.

Make sure there is enough to do on a rainy day—for your kids and yourself! Is there shopping nearby? Children's museums or indoor aquariums? Movie theaters? A bowling alley? Again, if you are planning your beach vacation in advance, you can access a lot of information about what's going on in the area beforehand, and plan, plan, plan!

Beaches Across the USA

There is not enough space to list and describe the many wonderful, intimate, pleasurable beaches that this country has to offer, so I have gathered here a bird's-eye view of the six main beach areas around the country, and the best times to visit.

• **New England, from Connecticut to Maine and all that lies in between—**Massachusetts hosts some of the country's most idyllic islands with pristine beaches, including Martha's Vineyard and Nantucket. The New England beach season is short if you want to swim and frolic in your bathing suit. June is still chilly; July warms up, but the ocean is still cool at 60 to 68 degrees. August is by far the best month. However, if you're flexible, September can be absolutely breathtaking. The days are shorter, but the water is still warm, the air is balmy, and the light is spectacular—plus, fewer crowds!

• **Mid-Atlantic States, Maryland, Virginia, Delaware, New Jersey, and New York—**The mid-Atlantic coast has many wide, sandy, and family-friendly beaches, as well as the fancy shores of the fabled southeast coast of Long Island, known as the Hamptons. Its beach season is quite similar to that of New England, extending from mid-June through early September, but the air and water temperatures are significantly warmer. When the ocean is 60 degrees in Maine and 65 degrees in Massachusetts, it's usually 70 degrees on Long Island or in Delaware.

• **The Great Lakes, including the shores of lakes Superior, Michigan, Huron, Erie, and Ontario—**The beaches along these magnificent lakes vary widely, with some offering rocky shores, others known for their wide stretches of sand, and still others changing daily with the tide. For this reason, it's best to consider each beach area individually, depending on how you want to spend your time. But one thing is for certain: The beach season is short and sweet, as most of the lakes are far north, and extends from late June through early September.

• ***Southeast Coast, including the Carolinas, Georgia, and the eastern coast of Florida***—These beaches are wide and varied, known for tidal pools, wild horses, and lots of fishing and clamming. Though the southeast coast has a longer beach season than New England and the mid-Atlantic states, swimming is comfortable only from May through October—after that, you'd better don a wet suit.

• ***The Gulf States, including the western coast of Florida, Alabama, Louisiana, and Texas***—The first thing you notice about the Gulf coast beaches is their flatness. The sand is denser and more packed, there are no dunes, and the shoreline seems to stretch forever, inching its way into the warm Gulf waters. Though winter does arrive and the air temperature drops below freezing in Alabama, Louisiana, and Texas, the water tends to stay fairly tepid, giving these Gulf state beaches a much longer season, extending from May through October. Florida's Gulf coast beaches, however, stay warm year-round (with summer being very warm), so you can plan a beach vacation to the Sunshine State no matter what time of year.

• ***California***—California's beaches vary widely, with those to the north being known for rocky, clifflike settings and those on the southern coast (from Santa Barbara on down to San Diego) known for wider, sandy shores. The northern waters rarely get above 65 degrees, whereas the Pacific below Los Angeles tends to stay fairly warm, at about 70 degrees throughout the year.

• ***Hawaii***—Hawaii is a whole other story. The beaches are sandy and warm, and the temperature of the water rarely gets below 75 degrees, regardless of the time of year, making Hawaii the perfect beach destination whatever the season.

New England

Ogunquit, Maine

One of my favorite beaches in the New England area is Ogunquit, Maine. Just forty-five miles north of Boston, this quiet little beach town has wide sandy beaches, the rocky coast Maine is known for, and absolutely pristine water. Established as a quiet artists' community, Ogunquit has a number of fascinating art galleries, private studios, and summer theater to visit and enjoy. People visit Ogunquit for short weekend trips or longer stays by the week or month.

> **Must See:** The Cliff House Resort Hotel
> **Must Do:** Walk to Perkins Cove
> **Must Try:** The lobster rolls, of course!

Contact www.maineguide.com/ogunquit.

Cape Cod, Massachusetts

Cape Cod is a great family beach resort area, with many towns dotting its shores. Though inns and hotels are few, there are many houses that can be rented on a weekly or biweekly basis. Located about thirty miles south of Boston, the Cape is a peninsula that juts into the sea and forms a hook at the state's southeast corner. When you first drive over one of two bridges, one of the first main towns you hit is Hyannis, made famous by the Kennedy family, who have had a compound there for many decades. Hyannis is one of the busiest and most populous towns on the Cape, which is either a plus or a minus, depending on what you're looking for. Hyannis offers plenty of affordable places to stay; go to www.hyannischamber.org for more information.

If Hyannis is too busy for you and you're looking for something quieter and a little more quaint, then check out Wellfleet, about fifteen miles east. You can often find better deals on rentals since Wellfleet is "north island." For more information regarding accommodations, both inns and rental houses, check out www.wellfleetchamber.com/index.html.

Still farther north, at the end of the peninsula, is Provincetown, which is an interesting mix of art galleries, restaurants, and nightclubs, as well as rocky and sandy beaches. A long-standing gay and lesbian travel destination, P-Town has an open, warm, and friendly atmosphere where everyone feels welcome. Even if you do not stay in Provincetown, you must plan to visit it if you're staying on Cape Cod. Provincetown is also a great place to visit in the fall, when rates are down, it's not so crowded, and you can enjoy a wonderful fall weekend by a fireplace in a cozy B&B. Contact www.capecodtravel.com for more information.

Must See: Pilgrim Monument and Provincetown Museum—includes exhibits on Pilgrims and the *Mayflower,* which dropped anchor here in 1620

Must Do: Take a seal-watching excursion from Chatham

Must Try: Triple Crown–winning clam chowder at Captain Parker's in Yarmouth

Narragansett Bay, Rhode Island

About an hour's drive south from Providence, Narragansett was established at the turn of the twentieth century as an elegant summer resort, known for its grand hotels, large estates, and smaller "cottages."

Still retaining its old-world charm, Narragansett is a friendly, accessible beach town with five beachfront state parks. Parking is easy and amenities are bountiful.

Rhode Island has many small covelike beach towns nestled along the coastline. A complete listing of all the beaches in Rhode Island can be found on www.visitri.com. This site also gives short descriptions of the beaches, indicating whether they are big, small, open to the public, and better for day-trippers, as well as whether they offer refreshment stands and facilities such as showers, bathrooms, and baby changing stations. Narragansett is suitable for both long-term stays of one, two, or four weeks, as well as short weekend stays. You can choose from plenty of accommodations, including extensive rental homes, inns, motels, and bed-and-breakfasts.

Must See: Galilee Fishing Village
Must Do: Visit Pettaquamscutt Cove National Wildlife Refuge
Must Try: Stuffies at George's waterfront restaurant

Mid-Atlantic Beaches

Fire Island, New York

Fire Island is a barrier island off the coast of Long Island, about fifty miles from New York City. It's made up of many different towns, each with its own distinct flair (the one thing they all have in common—pristine beaches on the gorgeous Atlantic Ocean). And while Fire Island has a long history as a gay resort destination, many families have been enjoying this quiet island for years. I have three favorites for families: Fair Harbor offers great rental houses, restaurants, bars, stores, marinas, and even a yacht club. Lonelyville, which was one of the first communities to be established on the island, still contains no stores, bars, or crowds. Everyone shuttles belongings by either bike or red wagon! And last but not least is Point o' Woods, where you feel as if you're living in a quaint turn-of-the-century country club. Its stores, kids' camps, tennis courts, fields, and the island's only train track make Point o' Woods a truly special place. Adding to the specialness of this beach area is its forestlike landscape, boardwalks, and huge fence with key-only access.

Although New York City dwellers come for weekends, if you are coming from outside the metropolitan area, I would recommend staying at least a week to enjoy Fire Island's special flavor. For extensive information about accommodations, activities, and dining, contact www.fireisland.com.

Must See: Sunken Forest, an enchanting maritime forest with a meandering boardwalk that kids will love

Must Do: Surfing—the waves are fantastic, especially after a storm!

Must Try: The Docks for a meal or drink at sunset

Cape May County, New Jersey

Cape May County is a peninsula located at the southernmost tip of New Jersey between the Atlantic Ocean and the Delaware Bay. Set along a thirty-mile stretch of clean, white sandy beaches along the Atlantic are the family-friendly resort towns of Ocean City, Sea Isle City, Avalon, Stone Harbor, the Wildwoods, and Cape May. Each of the towns offers a unique personality, an array of things to do with kids, and a super way to enjoy a beach vacation.

This stretch of the New Jersey coastline is sprinkled with quaint, family-oriented beaches that offer all styles of accommodations geared specifically to families. Most of the beaches are lined by boardwalks, reminding beachgoers of years gone by—all you need to fill in the mental picture is women in floor-length dresses and men in jumpsuit bathing costumes. Tour Victorian inns, enjoy an outdoor concert, spend a day at the park or zoo, and hunt for "Cape May diamonds." For all this family-friendly charm, Atlantic City is still in the vicinity (about thirty miles from the town of Cape May) if adults want to visit the casinos.

> ***Must See:*** The Cape May Lighthouse
> ***Must Do:*** Visit the Allen Family Farm's Blueberry Festival in Dennis Township
> ***Must Try:*** Cape May crab cakes

For more information about the specific towns in Cape May County, contact www.beachcomber.com.

Rehoboth, Delaware

The largest of Delaware's Atlantic resorts traces its origins to 1873, when the grounds of the Rehoboth Beach "Camp Meeting Association of the M.E. Church" were established. An air of the historic lingers in this special family-friendly beach resort town. Most families rent homes (many families who return summer after summer own second homes here), but there are a few inns and hotels that fit families well, including most of the major chains, some B&Bs, and smaller inns, as well as campgrounds.

The wide, sandy beaches are full of activities beyond sunbathing. Wherever your eye can roam, you will see young and old fishing, swimming, playing basketball and beach volleyball, and stretching their legs on the boardwalk that parallels the beach. Off the beach, Rehoboth offers a bandstand, shops of all kinds, including outlets, restaurants, amusements, and an active nightlife. Outside the summer season, Rehoboth Beach has some exciting events going on, including the Sea Witch Halloween Festival & Fiddler's Convention in late October and the world-famous Punkin Chunkin' contest in early November. This is also a popular tourism destination for gays and lesbians.

Must See: DiscoverSea Shipwreck Museum in nearby Delmarva

Must Do: Jungle Jim's Adventure World and Midway Speedway

Must Try: Funnel cake

For more specific information about the Rehoboth, Delaware, area, its accommodations, seasonal events, and other travel-related details, contact www.rehoboth.com.

The Great Lakes

One of my oldest friends grew up in Buffalo, New York, and spent her idyllic childhood summers on the shores of Lake Erie. While that shoreline is slowly changing, the once–sand-filled beaches becoming skinnier by the year, there are many other wonderful family beaches along the coasts of all of the five Great Lakes.

Mackinac Island, Michigan

Natives to Michigan call this historic island the only true "all-natural" theme park in America, since no motor vehicles are allowed and people are restricted to getting around by horse and buggy, bicycle, or foot. Situated in Lake Huron, the island radiates Victorian charm, especially in the cottages that line the bluffs. Each summer the population swells and high season begins, highlighted by the annual Lilac Festival and one of the largest "all-horse hitch" parades in the country. But that's not all. Families can enjoy all sorts of activities, including bike rides around the island, horse-drawn carriage rides, walking tours of the bluffs, and a visit to the Wings of Mackinac Butterfly Conservancy.

The summers are moderate, with cool mornings and warmer after-noons. Islanders suggest dressing in layers, shedding sweaters as the day progresses. By nightfall, sweaters are back on. In February, the Straits of

Mackinac freeze and Lake Huron is covered with ice. The average temperature in May is 50 degrees, but it reaches the seventies by July and August. Accommodations are plentiful, with a wide range of rental condos and houses, bed-and-breakfasts, and a few hotels. No camping is allowed on the island. For further information, go to www.mackinac.com.

> ***Must See:*** An all-horse hitch parade
>
> ***Must Do:*** Visit the Lilac Festival
>
> ***Must Try:*** The fudge

Grand Isle, Michigan

One of the most popular destinations for people who live in the Midwest is Grand Isle. Located in the northwest corner of Michigan's Lower Peninsula, along the shores of Lake Michigan's East Grand Traverse Bay, this beautiful shoreline offers great accommodations, activities for families, and fascinating sightseeing.

The Grand Traverse Resort Hotel offers a full-service spa, championship golf courses, children's programs, and shopping, and has been recognized by *Condé Nast Traveler* as a Top 20 Mainland Resort and Top 50 Worldwide Travel Destination. It is also known for its popular "Cub Camp" for kids ages six through twelve, as well as a licensed daycare in the Cub House for kids ages six months to five years. The staff all have backgrounds in teaching and recreation fields and are certified in first aid and CPR. They blend fun with learning for a great camp experience. Activities include sports clinics (golf, tennis, swimming, or fitness), sports activities (soccer, softball, volleyball, and field games), and theme activities, such as Time Machine, which allows campers to explore life in a different century.

Grand Traverse is home to several golf courses, including three eighteen-hole championship courses and a fourth in the planning stages. Everyone in the family can take lessons from top professionals.

The premier course, Spruce Run, was designed by William Newcomb. This par-seventy course winds along the hills overlooking East Grand Traverse Bay. The Wolverine was designed by Gary Player and opened in May 1999, his first signature course in Michigan. Just imagine: You can get in a leisurely game of golf while your kids are safe, sound, and having a ball Jet Skiing, sailing, or swimming. For more information on Grand Traverse Resort and Spa, call 800-748-0303 or visit their Web site at www.grandtraverseresort.com.

> ***Must See:*** Sleeping Bear Dunes National Lakeshore
>
> ***Must Do:*** Home-made pastries at the Sweetwater Cafe
>
> ***Must Try:*** Nauticat Catamaran breakfast cruise—especially for kids

Southeast Coast

Jekyll Island, Georgia

An exclusive haven for millionaires in the late nineteenth and early twentieth centuries, Jekyll Island is a 4,000-year-old barrier island made up of ten miles of uncrowded, unspoiled beach ready for a variety of activity. Find quiet solitude and communion with nature where the land meets the sea. Shell collecting is a popular island pastime for guests young and old, but the selection depends on the tides, wind, water currents, and time of year. It's not unusual to find buckets of specimens ranging from polished "olives" to knobbed whelks. You may even find live animals like hermit crabs and sand dollars. Though it's tempting to collect these interesting creatures, you can help preserve the shoreline by leaving them as you find them.

Your family may enjoy exploring more than twenty miles of winding trails through Jekyll's historic sites, beaches, marshes, and maritime forests. Bicycle rental is available next to the mini golf course as well as at many of the island's hotels and campgrounds. Jekyll

Island also offers ample opportunities for fishermen, from surf fishing off the beach to a relaxed outing on a freshwater lake. Offshore charter excursions can be booked from several operators at the Jekyll Harbor Marina. Crabbing and seining for shrimp are also popular activities.

With sixty-three holes of golf, Jekyll Island is Georgia's largest public golf resort. Three eighteen-hole courses and a historic nine-hole course offer an unmatched variety of golf experiences from one facility. The laid-back atmosphere and quality conditions have made Jekyll a popular group and tournament site, including the home of the U.S. Kids Golf World Championship (usually in February) and the Georgia State High School Championship.

The Jekyll Island Tennis Center, with thirteen clay courts, has been recognized as one of the finest municipal facilities in the country. Camps for every level are offered during the summer months, and personal lessons and small group clinics can be scheduled when you arrive.

Sea kayaking and canoeing are among the best ways to explore Jekyll's estuarial waters up close. Sea kayaks are lightweight and easily maneuvered.

Jekyll Island's nine hotels offer a variety of accommodations, from world-class resorts to budget motels. Choose from beachfront views of the Atlantic Ocean or riverside settings in the Historic Landmark District. Efficiencies, suites, villas, and B&B-style rooms are all available.

Must See: Jekyll Island Historic District
Must Do: Hear the Summer Music Festival
Must Try: Crab legs

For further information, visit www.jekyllisland.com.

Hilton Head Island, South Carolina

Hilton Head bills itself as a "year-round resort destination," and it certainly is. The largest barrier island between New York and Cuba, Hilton Head Island offers something for everyone. With a subtropical climate, the island enjoys great weather all year long, though swimming is best from May through October. Whether it's the lure of great golf, one of the finest beaches in the country, world-class tennis facilities, or water sports that brings you here, there's never a dull moment on Hilton Head. The island offers events from wine auctions to art festivals, Wing Fest to Chili Fest, and Gullah Festivals to auto shows. You also will find an enormous range of lodging and dining (casual and fine), as well as fantastic shopping. Of course, if you're simply looking for a peaceful beach to enjoy a good book, you've found the right place to get away from it all—for a while, anyway.

Are your kids interested in learning golf? The Golf Academy at Palmetto Dunes, a high-end resort hotel, offers top-notch clinics and private lessons from seasoned pros. At the Hilton OceanFront Resort you will find a terrific organized day of recreation for kids in the Seaside Adventures Club, which runs from Memorial Day through Labor Day. Kids can explore the beach, take a swim at the pool, play games, and do arts and crafts.

Hilton Head has its share of outlet malls. You can find Lenox, JCrew, Bass, Casual Corner, Vegas Golf, Nike, and even a Disney outlet store (Hilton Head Outlet II). Each area of Hilton Head Island also has its own unique and charming gift shops to browse through.

The unique low country of Hilton Head Island and the magic of Disney combined in 1996 to create a Disney Vacation Club Resort fashioned after a 1940s hunting and fishing lodge. Nestled among live oaks, some older than one hundred years, are 102 villas, a swimming pool, a small exercise room, a main lodge, and, one and a half miles away, a beach house and pool. The resort occupies fifteen acres adjacent to the Shelter Cove Harbour and Marina. As usual, Disney's Hilton Head Island Resort prides itself on its unique family programming—activities that children and their parents can enjoy together. This includes everything from painting T-shirts, to campfire marshmallow roasts and sing-alongs, to themed organized outings to nearby destinations, such as the historic city of Savannah, as well as programs designed for relationship building.

> **Must See:** The landmark red and white striped lighthouse for the best view of the island
>
> **Must Do:** Attend a Tuesday-night free concert and fireworks display (only in summer)
>
> **Must Try:** Taking a golf lesson at one of Hilton Head's many fine courses

Accommodations on Hilton Head run the gamut: from luxury hotels to budget motels, and many places in between. A large number of rental cottages, condos, and houses are also available. Contact www.hilton-headisland.com for a vast inventory of accommodation information.

Gulf States

Sandestin, Florida

On the Gulf coast of Florida is a secret hideaway resort called Sandestin. Sandestin has two distinct sides: the beach side on the Gulf of Mexico and the bay side on the Choctawhatchee Bay. The main center of Sandestin is the Village of Baytowne *(yes,* this is spelled correctly) Wharf—an entrancing city on the water with great stores. Indeed, shopping could definitely take one entire day—or, better yet, spread it out.

Activities include kayaking and canoeing in marsh areas, a night-

POOL PARTY!

*I*f the ocean, sand, and salt water are not your cup of tea, but you and yours do enjoy swimming, there can be no better place for your family to splash around than a well-designed hotel pool area. Here's a sampling of the fun that's out there:

- *Pointe Hilton, North Mountain, Phoenix, Arizona*—This all-suites resort is home to a huge pool area, complete with a lazy river for tubing and waterslides. If you want to spend time out of the water, a Wild West–themed mini golf course surrounds the pool, so you can dip in and cool off between holes.

- *Marriott Vacation Club, Horizons Resort, Orlando, Florida*—There is a pirate-themed, kid-friendly pool with daily dives for treasures. Adjacent to this pool is a mini water park—complete with cannon towers—that caters to the youngest pirates.

- *Grand Wailea Resort, Maui, Hawaii*—Steps away from the Pacific Ocean, this hotel is a kid's paradise as far as pool areas are concerned. Water elevators, waterslides, and water activities abound at this luxury property.

time visit to Captain Joe Lee's Tree House near the Bayside Marina, and fishing right nearby. Beachside activities include EuroBungy, a rock climbing wall, and the Dunes Putting Courses. Kids have so much to do, they will be flat-out exhausted by day's end!

There is also great golf to be enjoyed, with four golf courses offering junior golf programs and youth pricing that makes it affordable. The Dunes Putting Course offers after-dark play—a favorite among older kids who get restless at night. For kids ages six to twelve, the resort offers the Kidzone program, which has a full day of activities, in addition to half-day programs for ages four to five, and children's evenings out with pizza parties.

Accommodations are divided into five areas of the resort, Beachfront, Beachside, Village, Bayside, and Dockside. Contact the resort for further information regarding pricing and other amenities at www.sandestin.com.

> **Must See:** The Bark Avenue pet boutique, which has Halloween costumes for pets
> **Must Do:** Explore Jolee Island Nature Park and its playground
> **Must Try:** The saltwater taffy at the Candymaker, where you can watch it being made

Pleasure Beach, Alabama

The Gulf coast of Alabama offers beachgoers a hidden gem (well, not hidden to families who have been going here for years!), and you will not be disappointed if you decide to have your vacation here. Situated on the Gulf of Mexico, Alabama beaches have a long season—from May through October. Appropriately enough, the main beach is called Pleasure Beach, and it covers the coast's two towns of Gulf Shores and Orange Beach.

If you get tired of the beach, there is plenty of other excitement in the area. Kids will enjoy a visit to Fort Morgan and Fort Gaines and re-live the Battle of Mobile Bay, at which Confederate and Union forces fought for control of the port city. While on Dauphin Island, be sure to visit the Dauphin Island Sea Lab.

The Alabama Gulf coast is very family-friendly, and you do not have to spend a fortune on a house rental, hotel, or motel. There are also a multitude of activities—from lying on the beach, to playing a round of golf, to checking out all the adorable gift shops and boutiques, to parasailing, Jet Skiing, and, especially, deep-sea fishing—which the area is famous for. For more information, contact www.alagulfcoast.com.

Must See: The twin forts—Gaines and Morgan—for a reenactment of a Civil War battle

Must Do: Waterville, a park of waterslides and more

Must Try: Seafood gumbo at Bayside Grill

South Padre Island, Texas

This is perhaps the best-known Texas beach resort, located on the southern tip of Texas on the Gulf coast, with more than thirty miles of beautiful beaches. Although it attracts thousands of party-loving college kids in March for spring break, Padre Island is also a great family destination—just be careful when you are timing your vacation. South Padre's beach season extends from March through November. April brings the beginning of water sports, including windsurfing and Jet Skiing, which dominate. If your kids are active, they can take full advantage of these water sports and more; they can also enjoy parasailing, snorkeling, scuba diving, surfing, and fishing.

Younger kids may enjoy taking a sand castle–building lesson with "Sandy Feet," a local sand-sculpting legend, as well as dolphin watching and other water sports. Glass-bottom boat cruises are also popular. And if you want some real local flavor, try a sunset cruise during the Friday night "Fireworks over the Bay." Years ago, the fall was not such a busy time here, but now it's popular with serious fishermen and women.

In terms of accommodations, you can spend very little or a lot. Practically every major chain hotel is represented on the island, including the Radisson, the Sheraton, and La Quinta. Dozens of condos for rent are scattered across the island (contact www.discoverourtown.com).

> **Must See:** Sea Turtle, Inc.
>
> **Must Do:** Schlitterbahn Beach Waterpark
>
> **Must Try:** Bubba's Bar-B-Que

California

Stinson Beach

Stinson Beach is one of Northern California's most treasured state parks. As you come over the Golden Gate Bridge and off Route 1, you will be amazed at the magnificent beauty around you. Ramble down the cliffs onto the beach area below. Three and a half miles of sand give plenty of access to swimmers, surfers, and sunbathers. The fifty-one-acre park adjacent to the beach offers more than one hundred picnic tables (some with grills—all available on a first-come basis). A snack bar is open April through September. The park is open until sunset.

> **Must See:** A play at Shakespeare at the Beach
>
> **Must Do:** Visit the Muir Woods filled with majestic redwood trees, some more than five hundred years old
>
> **Must Try:** To climb the Point Reyes Lighthouse, built in 1970, atop a 308-step walkway

Monterey

Monterey, approximately forty miles south of San Francisco, is a family-fun beach town a day trip from San Francisco or a weekend destination from other parts of California. Though not a beach town meant for sun-bathing and swimming, Monterey offers kids and adults tons to do and see. If your family is into the outdoors, you can meander along a twenty-nine-mile trail up the Monterey Peninsula coastline or hike through Garrapata State Park. The rocky shoreline, redwood canyons, and soaring mountains are breathtaking. Families can rent kayaks and paddle around the bountiful Monterey Bay, catch sight of seals, gaze down at tide pools, and take in the rocky coastline looming above. Those who love animals have a number of ways to enjoy wildlife, including Wild Things Animal Park in nearby Salinas, home to lions, tigers, and elephants, as well as many other animals. The Monterey Bay Aquarium is also a must-see destination. Kids can don scuba gear and experience life under the sea, pet sharks and rays, and much more. If you're heading to the aquarium, make sure you stop and enjoy some of the great restaurants, sites, and souvenir shops of Cannery Row. Older kids and parents will appreciate a visit to the National Steinbeck Center. For more information, contact www.monterey.org.

Must See: Monterey Bay Aquarium

Must Do: Close Encounter with a giraffe or elephant at Wild Things Animal Park

Must Try: A stroll through Cannery Row

Mother's Beach

This quaint beach feels like an anomaly so close to the circuslike boardwalk scene of nearby Venice Beach. But Mother's Beach is aptly named, as it is tranquil and peaceful even on busy days. A good beach for a day trip from anywhere in Southern California, there are plenty of parks, easy dining spots, and amenities, including bathrooms, showers, and baby changing stations.

Must See: Seals frolicking in the harbor

Must Do: Go to a free summer concert at the outdoor ampitheater

Must Try: A relaxing drink at the Cheesecake Factory, while your kids enjoy themselves at the playground on the beach right across from you

Dana Point

This family beach is located in Orange County, near San Juan Capistrano, midway between Los Angeles and San Diego. Known for its Festival of the Whales each March, it is a fabulous place to bring your family—for a day trip if you live within driving distance or a day excursion if you are visiting another part of California. Kids will love the whale-watching trips out into the Pacific, as well as the boat parades and other festivities.

> **Must See:** Festival of the Whales
> **Must Do:** Scenic bike tour along the ocean's edge
> **Must Try:** Lunch at the Train Station, a restaurant at which a train actually pulls into the station!

San Diego

Of course, hundreds of beaches line the coast of California; it would take me days to list them all. With that in mind, I have highlighted just a few of my top favorites. Starting in the south, San Diego is a must. Recently named the number-one family destination by several travel industry experts including *Travel & Leisure* magazine, San Diego offers any and all families a marvelous vacation experience. Its climate—warm and dry twelve months of the year—makes it a perfect destination year-round.

San Diego has some of California's most pristine sandy beaches. Whereas much of Northern California's beaches are lined with rocky terrain and the Los Angeles beaches tend to be a bit dirty and overcrowded, San Diego's shores are wide and open and perfect for families to enjoy. Whether you want the splendid openness of Coronado or the busy boardwalk activities of Mission Bay, San Diego has something for any family. Outside the beach, you and your family will find Sea World, as well as La Jolla's fancy shopping. Over the last ten years, downtown San Diego has spent a lot of time and money rebuilding its Old Town district, which boasts fabulous Mexican food; its Gaslamp Quarter, home of several great jazz clubs, including Croce's of Jim Croce fame; and its Mission Hills area, where you can find more cosmopolitan dining and shopping.

The San Diego Zoo is one of the world's finest zoos, where animals live in too-good-to-be-true natural settings and kids learn through mere observation.

Accommodations are ubiquitous and range from luxury to budget hotels, inns, and motels. Contact www.sandiego.org.

Must See: Balboa Park

Must Do: Visit the San Diego Zoo

Must Try: Mexican food in Old Town

Once in a Lifetime Beach Vacation:

Hawaii

I have to be honest: Hawaii is one of my favorite destinations of all time. But, obviously, it's not easy to get to, and this can make it expensive. Despite these challenges, Hawaii is my choice for a "once in a lifetime" beach vacation.

My family and I have visited the islands of Hawaii more than ten times, and each visit we experience something new and equally memory making. Though Hawaii seems far away and does require long air travel, it has so much to offer in terms of activities, sightseeing, accommodations, and dining that the time and cost are definitely worth it.

Hawaii is an archipelago made up of eight small and not-so-small islands; its six main islands are Hawaii (the Big Island), Oahu, Maui, Kauai, Lanai, and Molokai. Because of the distance, you may want to make your trip at least six or seven days or longer if possible to compensate for jet lag, time difference, and travel fatigue. Here I am going to focus on the islands of Maui and Kauai—two favorites for family trips.

Maui

Maui is a great place for families to visit. For years its slogan has been Maui Loves Kids, and there is so much for them to do. The Goofy Foot Surf School in Lahaina is the ideal place to get on a board. You can also bike down a volcano on this island. And if none of these activities tickles your fancy, you can simply sit at the beach and enjoy the warm Pacific Ocean.

You will want to rent a car so you can take a drive out to see the Haleakala Crater, Hana, and Upcountry Maui. On your way, you will see waterfalls and scenic views from atop a dormant volcano, as well as local flora and fauna.

Beyond driving tours, there is still more to do on Maui. Check out the beach scene in Paia, the boutiques and galleries of Makawao, and the beautiful botanical garden in Kula. The kids in particular will love the Keiki (Children's) Petting Zoo and the cowboy life at Ulupalakua Ranch.

Families who want to add an element of soft adventure can try a hike in and out of Haleakala Crater, with its strange landscapes and natural curiosities. People "do the crater" as a vigorous day hike or with an overnight in a cabin or campground. You can learn to scuba dive together on Maui and complete the course with an unforgettable experience in underwater "cathedrals" on the back side of Lanai.

Maui doesn't exclude the family members who may not feel ready to strap on hiking boots or swim fins. A helicopter will take the whole family farther than feet dare go. Then there's the Maui Ocean Center's state-of-the-art aquarium, which lets the whole family experience and learn about the scuba divers' world from the comfort of shore.

Maui has lots of ways to slip in an educational experience for yourselves and your kids. The Maui Tropical Plantation is 112-acre working farm set up with a tram, displays, and demonstrations about the fruit crops and flowers that are indigenous to this tropical climate.

Maui has a number of family-friendly options for accommodations. There is an Embassy Suites hotel in Kaanapali that offers a terrific way to spread out while you stretch your travel dollar. Also, many of the resort communities rent condominiums as well as hotel rooms, including the Kapalua and Waleia hotels, so you can have the convenience of kitchen facilities and an extra room or two.

Kauai

Kauai is absolutely breathtaking. Since it is the least developed of the four major Hawaiian islands, it offers fewer accommodations options, with several budget-minded hotel and motels in the city itself, as well as a few in Poipu, the main beach resort area. Choose from a number of moderate inns, such as the Garden Island, as well as a few high-end resorts, including a Hyatt, Marriott, and Radisson. Bed-and-breakfasts, camping, and vacation rentals are also available. Contact www.kauai-hawaii.com for further information. You will fly into Lihue, the island's capital.

Kauai is where my family goes to really be active and try every sport Hawaii has to offer. Like Maui, it too has a dormant volcanic peak, Mt. Waialeale, as well as challenging cliffs you can hike that overlook the ocean. Many wonderful nonchallenging activities are available to delight your entire family. Take a look at these options:

All-Terrain Vehicle (ATV) Excursions

Venture into Kauai's lush, tropical paradise on the back of a fully automatic, easy-to-use all-terrain vehicle. Daily ATV expeditions through the gorgeous mountains of Kauai's south side, winding through thick vegetation and rugged terrain to secluded waterfalls, will get your blood pumping. Families will enjoy the "Mud Bug" vehicle. Guests can drive the fully automatic off-road vehicle on any of the adventure tours with the entire family riding along in the same vehicle. This activity is suitable for kids five years old and up.

Bicycle Downhill Canyon to Coast

Enjoy a fun, exciting bike ride that takes you from the rim of the famed Waimea Canyon down twelve miles of smooth, winding blacktop to the shore of the blue Pacific. Riders can choose between a four-hour sunrise or three-and-a-half-hour sunset ride. Whether you decide to see the sunrise over Waimea Canyon or the sunset over Niihau, this tour is spectacular. Ride through one of the most beautiful and interesting places on the planet on comfortable bikes with wide saddles and high handlebars. Of course, you'll stop along the way for photos and a narrative on history, culture, folklore, and legends. This activity is best suited for kids ten and up.

Helicopter Tours

Many of the most exquisite places on Kauai are inaccessible by car. For this reason, a helicopter tour is an unbeatable way to see the Garden Island. Kauai is breathtakingly beautiful from the air, with rolling hills and valleys on the eastern shore and majestic mountains on the west. What you'll see is beyond your fantasies—a mountain goat poised for an instant in a ravine, a white bird gliding against the dark green cliffs, a sudden rainbow in the mist. Perhaps you'll see a tower-like waterfall hanging like a slender silver ribbon through trees and rocks, or a curve of pure white sand at the base of the purple and gold Napali cliffs. You'll yearn to go up again. This activity is suitable for all ages, but children must weigh at least forty pounds to account for the weight balance on board.

Gay & Robinson Sugar Plantation Tours

Sugar plantations were the driving force in shaping territorial Hawaii (1898–1959), and the archipelago's green fields of cane and pineapple bring visitors a sense of this agricultural history. Ironically, because of tourism today pineapple and sugarcane fields are rapidly disappearing. You can take a tour of an authentic Hawaiian sugar plantation—including both field and factory operations—and immerse yourself in a world seldom seen by visitors and residents. You'll learn about the unique history and culture of the only sugar plantation still operating on Kauai.

Koloa Heritage Trail

The new four-mile Koloa Heritage Trail, created by the Poipu Beach Resort Association (PBRA), features twelve different stops with historical and cultural information about each location on bronze-cast signs. The trail, also called "Ka Ala Hele Waiwai Ho'oilina O Koloa" in Hawaiian, is a self-guided tour that you can explore by foot, bicycle, or automobile. Stops along the trail in Koloa Town include the sugar monument, Yamamoto Store, Koloa Hotel, Koloa Jodo Mission, and Koloa Missionary Church.

Myths and Legends Tour

To the Polynesians, who had no written language, storytelling had special significance. The stories preserved their history and culture. Tales of romance, bravery, tragedy, and heroism revealed a deep respect for and understanding of the natural environment. Stories were used to teach children the lessons of life, to reinforce values in adults, and to pass on the wisdom of the elders. For a full day, hear tales of bravery and passion from a gifted storyteller as you tour the lush North Shore.

Hiking

With more than half of Kauai made up of forestland, this island is a hiker's paradise. Whether you want to hike the scenic Kalalau Trail along the Napali coast or Waimea Canyon, Kauai is a wonderful maze of interesting trails, hidden waterfalls, and archeological mystery. You can take a guided tour with a geologist to learn more about the island up close or venture out with a friend at your own leisurely pace.

Horseback Riding

A horseback ride through emerald pastures to secluded waterfalls and vistas offers a peaceful yet exciting way to experience Kauai's *paniolo* (cowboy) lifestyle and also to get a rare look at Kauai's North Shore backcountry. Even if you've never been on a horse before, you can feel secure that your horse, which has made the trip many times, knows the trail well and will confidently follow your guide. You can enjoy the perfect Hawaiian setting with a picnic and swim at the base of a waterfall or experience the adventure of a genuine cattle drive.

Kayak Adventures

The Hanalei River weaves through the Hanalei National Wildlife Refuge, home to endangered native water birds, such as the Hawaiian coot, the black-necked stilt, the Koloa duck, and the gallinule. Today, large green heart-shaped leaves of taro carpet the valley, and the abundant crop supplies about half of Hawaii's poi. Guided tours of the land, water, fauna, and flora offer safe family entertainment. You'll also catch views of Makana Peak and the sweeping Pacific Ocean.

Or you might take a guided kayak adventure up the beautiful Huleia River. You'll see jumping fish, rare birds, ancient taro fields, the legendary Menehune Fishpond, magnificent Haupu Ridge, and the magical Kaukaohu. During your trip, you will land on privately owned Kipu Ranch and hike through a tropical forest that has a towering canopy of exotic trees and an explosion of tropical flowers. The Huleia River and Kipu Ranch are so remote and distinctly tropical that many movies have been filmed there, including *Six Days Seven Nights, Raiders of the Lost Ark,* and *Jurassic Park.*

Wailua River

A guided tour on the Wailua River is a wonderful adventure for the whole family, combining idyllic paddling and a hike to a remote bridal veil waterfall. The Wailua River became the center of activity for early Hawaiians and is known as one of Hawaii's most sacred places. It is said that at night, one can still hear ancient drums thunder in concert with the nearby surf. The trail leading to the secret waterfall is a lively "greenhouse" where flowers, brooks, and ferns abound. The pace of this tour is tranquil and unhurried, so that you can fully experience the life and natural history of this mystical land.

Movie Tours

If movies are your thing, you are sure to enjoy a journey to the filming locations of some of Hollywood's most memorable features in a four-by-four van with no more than eleven guests. As you visit each film set, you watch the actual movie on a large TV screen with built-in surround sound system. The tour visits the sets of *Jurassic Park, Six Days Seven Nights, Blue Hawaii, South Pacific, Honeymoon in Vegas,* and many other films and TV shows.

Olokele Canyon Overlook Tour

This morning tour is conducted in an extended-cab truck. Local tour guides take you behind locked gates and treat you to a world seldom seen by visitors and residents. Visitors will learn about the rich sugar history of Gay & Robinson's Makaweli property, which includes their sugar plantation and Makaweli Ranch, with a startling view of Waimea Canyon's eastern rim. Makaweli Ranch is notable for its Durham Shorthorn cattle, originally brought to the property by the Sinclair family in 1865. And the sugar fields are some of the highest yielding in the world.

River Boat Cruise

A river cruise up to the famous Fern Grotto is an excellent way to learn how Hawaiian royalty lived. Boat operators share the fascinating legends of the area, and family members entertain with Hawaiian songs, old and new. In this tropical jungle setting, nature has formed a natural amphitheater with remarkable acoustics. The river and its surrounding land were once part of the royal grounds.

Surfing

Surf's up! And on Kauai there is always perfect surf to learn on. From long-board to short-board surfing, small-wave hot doggin' to big-wave riding, instructors are more than happy to find an excuse to get in the water and teach. You are guaranteed to stand during your first lesson.

CONSIDER THE BEACH OFF-SEASON

*D*on't shelve your swimsuit! Just because it's not summer doesn't mean the beach is off-limits. In fact, there are loads of reasons—from the price to the weather—to visit the ocean even during the off-season. Beach resort areas tend to have short seasons (with the exception of Hawaii and Florida), and hotel and resort operators often offer discounts off-season. For this reason, it's best to do your prep work and find out the average room rates in the area you're going to. Take a look at these examples:

• ***The Grand Wailea Resort, Maui, Hawaii*—**This wonderful resort offers a travel bargain that allows guests who stay two nights to receive the third night free. If you have enough time to stay for a week, pay for the first four nights, and nights five and six are complimentary. They also toss in a free daily breakfast buffet for two with the longer hotel stay. The island of Maui is beautiful year-round.

• ***Newport, Rhode Island*—**For a bargain rate, you can enjoy two midweek nights of luxury accommodations, gourmet breakfast, champagne, and wine and cheese. This beach community is home to terrific sailing and boating and is absolutely beautiful in the fall. (www.GoNewport.com)

• ***Marquis Los Cabos Golf Resort and Spa, Cabo San Lucas, Mexico*—**You can take advantage of this resort's fall travel offer—purchase one room, and receive 50 percent off a second. Choose from sport fishing, golf, or old-fashioned rest and relaxation at the beach at this great vacation spot.

Of course, "off-season" varies with location. Off-season for New England is midwinter, and off-season for the Caribbean is midsummer. You can find deals on beach vacations yourself by using online search engines, combing the Sunday newspaper, or signing up for one of many travel websites, such as TravelZoo.com.

Lessons are conducted on soft foam boards and emphasize safe surfing and wave dynamics. For the more experienced, a selection of short and long fiberglass boards are available. And what would a trip to Hawaii be without giving surfing a try?

For information about visiting Hawaii, contact www.gohawaii.com. For further information about traveling to Kauai, visit www.kauai-hawaii.com.

Checklist for Beach Vacations

- ❑ Decide if you are willing to travel off-season or high season.
- ❑ Pack for both good and inclement weather.
- ❑ Research your accommodations options and decide on a hotel, motel, B&B, rental condo, or house.
- ❑ Bring any supplies that a rental house may not provide, including food, towels, linens, and beach towels.
- ❑ Make sure you know your accommodations. If they advertise "beachfront," make sure you know exactly what that means. Do you get a glimpse of the ocean or beach, or can you walk to the beach from the property?

• Golden Moment Rule #5 •

Slow Down

*T*here is a reason why native islanders move more slowly than the rest of us: island life is slow. When on a beach vacation in particular, slow down and listen to the hum of the waves.

❑ Research the special events, activities, and entertainment available during your stay.

❑ Sign up for any events or activities that you are interested in participating in that require advance booking or reservations.

Has a beach vacation beckoned, or are you still trying to put your finger on the perfect destination? Look ahead: Here comes an array of winter wonderland trips—for everyone!

. SIX .

Winter Holidays and Trips for Cool Weather

In the middle of winter, the concept of a cold-weather vacation can be less than appealing. However, every time I take one I am thrilled with the results. Winter trips provide a real pick-me-up in what can be a gray, gloomy season. Although I wouldn't call myself a skier by nature, I certainly enjoy the sport once I am participating in it, and I've had some magical moments on the slopes. Skiing down a sunny mountain with my husband and two kids, I begin thinking, "It really doesn't get much better than this."

That said, it can be intimidating to tackle a winter trip with your kids for the first time. Since ski trips in particular can be expensive, many families put off introducing their kids to the joy and thrill of skiing and snowboarding. Though these activities do cost money, there are ways to maximize your travel dollar.

So when the weather begins to change, resist the urge to head indoors and instead discover the plentitude of pleasures in the winter wonderlands all over this magnificent country of ours. Whether you and your family enjoy skiing and snowboarding or not, you can still find tons of fun in a snowy landscape. Have you ever wanted to learn how to skate? Did you know it's easier to learn on hockey skates than figure skates? When was the last time you plunked yourself down on a sled and slid down a hill? Another sport that has become popular is snowshoeing, which can be enjoyed at any skill level. So remember that when the temperature drops, it's not just ski season that has happened upon us! There's a reason we want our kids to play outdoors in the winter: Yes, they will definitely sleep better, but they also will have a blast, and so will you! Before considering the where of your winter vacation, take a look at the fun activities that you can find in many of the destinations described in this chapter.

Winter Activities for Everyone

Winter trips tend to be about getting outside and being active, combined with snuggling by a warm fire, sipping cocoa. Here is a brief overview of sports and activities that you can enjoy in many winter vacation destinations:

- *Skiing*—This is the number-one activity for winter-weather lovers, and now there are plenty of mountains and resorts that cater to families—at all skill levels.

- *Snowboarding*—Ten years ago this sport barely existed, and now we can't imagine a mountain without boarders. You can sign kids up for snowboarding lessons, and I recommend that you do so if they want to try it.

- *Sledding*—From sliding down the bunny slope to tobaggoning down a full-size hill, sledding can be a wonderful way to spend family time.

• ***Skating***—Indoors or outdoors, skating is not only a wonderful sport to watch but is fun to do as well.

• ***Snowshoeing***—Though people have been using snowshoes for ages, it seems all the winter-wear catalogs have just recently caught on to the popularity of this sport. Snowshoes now come in all varieties of sizes, weights, and shapes. Kids will love to stomp around in the snow!

• ***Cross-country or "Nordic" skiing***—This sport is great exercise and can be enjoyed regardless of skill level. As you will note, many of this country's premier downhill ski destinations also offer both exciting and easy trails for Nordic skiing.

Not all members of your family may want to participate in outdoor winter sports. As you peruse the many destinations I describe, consider your family's interests beyond the outdoors. If you think your family would like a break from skiing or other outdoor activities while away, consider the areas that offer more shopping, dining, and entertainment than others. Many resorts also have indoor pools, Jacuzzis, tennis, game rooms, and spa services to keep your mind and body active if you don't particularly like winter outdoor sports and recreation. Before booking, be sure the resort or ski area offers other activities and points of interest.

Ski Trips—Some Advice

When taking your family on a ski trip, keep these considerations in mind:

Equipment

Remember that kids grow, and their bodies change from the end of one ski season to the beginning of another. Make sure that their equipment is appropriate for their current size and weight. Although helmets may not be "cool," I insist on them for my kids and many mountains now require them. If you start your kids off with helmets when they are young, they are much more likely to make a helmet a habit.

Lessons

I am a big believer in leaving the teaching to the professionals. Winter sports such as skiing, snowboarding, and skating require certain skills. If your kids are just learning and you are a little rusty, everyone should take at least one lesson. This helps you to refresh skills, get a feel of the skis or skates under your feet, and get a mini tour of the mountain. All mountain resorts offer private lessons, clinics, and assorted packages. The best family destinations specialize in teaching kids in a safe, supportive environment. Call ahead during peak seasons to make sure that spaces are reserved for your kids. Not only will they be learning safely, but you can enjoy some adult time on the slopes.

Clothing

The rule of thumb with skiing is to layer. Light but warm clothes made of microfiber can be worn under jackets and snow pants. Gone are the days of layering with wool and cotton, which get hot and wet! I keep a box just for ski clothes in the garage and toss things that will work into it throughout the year. Here are some items you cannot do without:

- Hats, gloves, mittens, and liners from a ski shop or sporting good store
- Long underwear in microfiber, silk, or some blend of the two
- Turtlenecks
- Fleece

- Warm after-ski boots
- Snow pants and jackets
- Protective eyewear, such as goggles
- Helmets—yes! For everyone!
- Bathing suits for pool or Jacuzzi

Accommodations

If you are looking for a more economical ski vacation, renting a house or condo is a terrific way to stretch your money. Most vacation homes include a full kitchen, extra space to sleep more people, and washers

SKIING IS EXPENSIVE

*A*lthough the price of a ski or winter vacation may take you by surprise at first, consider how much value you are getting. Ski resorts run only a limited number of months per year, and a lot of equipment, maintenance, and staff go into running a ski resort. These elements combine to drive up the cost of lift tickets, rental equipment, and sometimes accommodations, making a winter trip at a ski resort a relatively expensive proposition. To get the most for your travel dollar, make sure to look into multiday lift tickets and packages that include lessons, rentals, and lift tickets. Keep in mind:

- Holidays are the most expensive times to go skiing.
- Most ski resorts offer midweek specials and discounts.
- Rates are lower—for both accommodations and lift tickets—pre- and postseason.
- Search websites for special ski packages.
- Some ski resorts, especially in Utah, offer free lift tickets on the day you arrive—so save your boarding pass!

and dryers. But always inquire how far the condo is from the mountain; some rental places may be situated too far and are therefore too inconvenient. Often you can find deals if you book early.

Hitting the Slopes: Destinations

The West

From California to Colorado and all points in between, the western areas of the United States offer superior conditions for skiing. If you like sunny and dry and lots of powder, check out these ski destinations.

California

California is famous for everything from movie stars, to beaches, to wine country, and it has great skiing, too! With a temperate climate, California offers weather for skiing that is never too cold and often is dry and sunny, making it great for young skiers. These are a few of the Golden State ski areas that I like the most:

• *Mammoth Mountain (www.mammothmountain.com)* is a day trip from Los Angeles, San Francisco, Las Vegas, and San Diego. Located in the eastern Sierras, Mammoth is a quaint ski town with a variety of accommodations to suit every budget and every level of service desired. There are two different ski schools, including one that caters to young kids and offers two- to four-hour lessons. Women can participate in female-only ski seminars throughout the season, too.

• *Lake Tahoe (www.visitinglaketahoe.com)* is a massive area with all kinds of skiing and snowboarding options and several distinct resorts. Mt. Rose is a smaller facility that offers programs ranging from "skills to thrills" to "Rosebuds kids program for boarders and skiers."

Squaw Valley offers highly discounted packages for early season, which include a night for a condo and lift tickets.

• **Big Bear (www.bigbearmountain.com)** is a short drive from Los Angeles and is home to both Bear Mountain and Snow Summit. In less than two hours, you can leave the city and be on the slopes. These ski areas feature a freestyle park, jumps, and traditional downhill runs. Accommodations are affordable, and it is a refreshing weekend escape from L.A. during the winter months.

Jackson Hole, Wyoming

Jackson Hole is a classic ski resort that has been known in the past for its action-packed, challenging downhill runs. Though it still has all of those, the ski resort has developed a phenomenal program for kids of all ages. Offering expert instruction for all-level skiers and boarders, there are many options for getting kids on—and off—the slopes. For the youngest skiers, Cody House Kids Ranch is an all-inclusive ski in/ski out children's facility that was named the number-one ski school for kids by *Good Skiing and Snowboarding Guide* in 2005. The Cody House Kids Ranch is a 106,000-square-foot building that houses day care for children ages six months and up, as well as all youth rentals and Mountain Sports School product registration. There is an adventure playground where kids can ski through secret tree trails, explore new terrain, and get up close and personal with wildlife.

The charming Fort Wyoming western playground, adjacent to the Kids Ranch, teaches little kids how to ski through the use of western characters and a magic carpet, and a gentle, protected slope provides the perfect environment.

For older kids, especially if they are adrenaline junkies like mine, the Team Extreme program is great. It is for kids twelve to seventeen and focuses on mountain orientation, versatility, steeps, and backcountry tours. A terrain park and superpipe are accessible for most skill levels. These experiences are led by incredibly cool athletes and operate seasonally.

Lodging ranges from the quaint B&B to small inns, and rental condos are also available. For those of you who are into the high life, the Four Seasons recently opened the only ski in/ski out resorts in Jackson Hole. Once difficult to reach, Jackson Hole is now much easier to get to thanks to a brand-new airport. If you'd like to try out Jackson Hole for a winter trip, keep in mind that it is known for very changeable weather and cold winter temperatures that average 10 to 35 degrees. For more information, contact www.jacksonhole.com.

Colorado

If you're looking for great family-friendly ski options, you'll be hard-pressed to find anyplace better than Colorado, where fresh snow falls from November through April. Though the winter temperatures are on average below freezing, the dry and sunny climate makes for comfortable ski conditions. Colorado is known for high-end mountains such as Vail and Aspen, but there are plenty of family-friendly places to ski, as well. Here are just a few of the great resorts that the Centennial State has to offer:

• *Club Med Crested Butte (www.clubmed.com)* is an all-inclusive family winter sports resort. Ski or snowboard on eighty-eight different slopes while enjoying the casual comfort of a Club Med village. Meals, lift tickets, lessons, and activities are all included in the price of a family package.

• *The Wyndham Peaks and Resort in Telluride (www.wyndham.com)* is a luxurious property with a terrific deal for families— kids eat, stay, snowboard, and ski free when accompanied by a paying adult. The Golden Door Spa is also located at this resort, and it is the perfect place to have your aches and pains massaged away after a day on the slopes.

• *Breckenridge (www.breckenridge.snow.com)* is the home of four interconnected peaks where kids and adults can ski, snowboard, skate, and go for sleigh rides, as well as try helicopter skiing and cross-country skiing. Kids can learn to ski at their own pace in either groups or private lessons, or can take their ski skills up a notch by participating in an array of specialty programs such as Park and Pipe, Adaptive, Bombers, and Telemarking. Boasting an average of three hundred days of sunshine, this mountain town makes outdoor winter sports comfortable and pleasant, as well as challenging. As one of Colorado's bigger ski towns, Breckenridge offers extensive accommodation options at hotels and lodges, bed-and-breakfasts, rental condos, and houses.

• *Steamboat Ski & Resort Corporation (www.steamboat. com)* is a complete mountain range made up of six peaks. This laidback, friendly town has a distinct cowboy flair that immediately sets it apart. Its ski program for kids is exceptional, as is the Billy Kidd Performance Center, founded by the Olympic medal–winning skier. Adults and kids of all ages and skill levels can learn to apply Olympic training methods and techniques to their skiing. The Kids Vacation Center offers day and evening activities for kids ages six months through kindergarten, child care, as well as incentives such as free rentals for kids with each five-day adult rental. After skiing and boarding, your whole family will enjoy a stroll through the quaint town of shops, restaurants, and boutiques. Like Breckenridge, Steamboat enjoys many sunny days of fairly mild winter weather. Its winter ski season extends from late November through early April.

Park City, Utah

Sunny, dry, and with dependable snowfall, Park City is a premier ski and winter resort destination. Park City is divided into a few main areas—Deer Valley (its own resort), Park City, and The Canyon (a resort). They are all family-friendly, with easy transportation between them, including buses to get you to and from slopes. There is also great shopping in all the resort areas. Deer Valley offers an array of condominiums, townhouses, and private homes, with a huge variety of prices, as well as deluxe and moderate hotels. Many resorts offer package deals that include lift tickets. Contact www.skiparkcityutah.net for more information.

Sun Valley/Ketchum, Idaho

Sun Valley, also known for its dry, sunny climate, is really made up of three small towns that include Ketchum, where the locals live and you will find charming restaurants and shops; the town of Sun Valley, which is dominated by the Sun Valley Resort but also contains smaller inns and hotels, as well as restaurants; and Warm Springs, which is where the mountain is. Even if you're staying at the Sun Valley resort, you can take a free bus to Warm Springs to get to the mountain.

Not every Sun Valley winter activity requires a lift ticket. The surrounding area supplies visitors with an endless variety of spectacular scenery and sporting diversions. You can spend a day mushing a pack of huskies, turn a few circles at the famed Sun Valley ice rink, cuddle up in a cozy yurt, or hop a horse-drawn sleigh for a hearty dinner at the legendary Trail Creek Cabin. Snowmobiles provide an easy means to explore the incredible backcountry, and the devoted will still be fishing the local rivers in mid-December. With so much to occupy your time, a return trip to Sun Valley may be necessary. Accommodations are plentiful. Go to www.sunvalley.com for more information.

Taos, New Mexico

Taos is actually a blend of several close-knit communities that, together, provide visitors with a virtual cultural cornucopia—a mix of Anglo, American Indian, and Spanish cultures. Not so very long ago, miners, trappers, cattlemen, and sheepherders circled Wheeler Peak, the highest peak in New Mexico at 13,161 feet, following the faint lines of ancient footpaths to remote villages. The same mountains that used to divide cultures now provide a winter playground for all called the Enchanted Circle.

Activities abound. Snowshoe and cross-country ski enthusiasts enjoy the backcountry trails and meadows in Carson National Forest and the groomed trails at the Enchanted Forest Cross-Country Ski Area. Anglers explore the frozen surface of Eagle Nest Lake and try their hand at landing Kokanee salmon and rainbow and cutthroat trout. For fast and furious fun in the snow, you can take a guided snowmobile trip through the valleys and mountains, where you can see for miles and miles.

Taos contains a seemingly endless supply of opportunities to explore the region. Visit Taos Pueblo and you will find an ancient living Indian village that has stood unchanged for centuries. Explore historic Taos Plaza and its side streets, where you can see old adobe buildings that now house shops and galleries but were once the homes of some of Taos's leading citizens, Kit Carson among them. You might also set off on a mountain trail on skis, horseback, bike, or your own two feet. Or ride the bucking Rio Grande in a raft or kayak.

Whether you are a beginning or an expert skier, the four resorts of Taos, Red River, Sipapu, and Angel Fire are comfortable and family-friendly and provide the best skiing possible. You can choose from staying on the mountain or in town. Some families prefer being on the mountain for the ease and convenience to daily skiing. But if your family is interested in balancing skiing with some historical and cultural activities, then you might prefer to stay closer to town. Taos is really a

LOOK IN THE MIRROR

*L*ooking to enjoy a great ski vacation while the kids keep busy with their own winter fun? The **Mirror Lake Inn** (www.mirrorlakeinn.com) at Lake Placid, New York, has a children's holiday program that fits the bill perfectly. The daylong schedule of activities includes snow-cave making, Adirondack arts and crafts, and dance and music lessons. The holiday program takes place in the Whiteface Club and Resort boathouse, adjacent to the Whiteface Mountain ski area. The program includes most activities, but for an additional charge kids can take part in dogsled rides, ice fishing, and cross-country skiing with professional guides. And they will experience a special thrill knowing that they are skiing, skating, or sledding on the same terrain as the 1980 Winter Olympics!

magical place for you and your family to experience a winter wonderland adventure in unique desert surroundings. Contact www.skitaos.org for more information.

New England

Yes, it gets cold there, but there may be no better place than northern New England for family skiing. A smorgasbord of family ski areas and wonderful resorts and inns dot the rolling hills and mountains of Vermont, New Hampshire, and Maine. As you will see below, Vermont in particular has a great number of ski destinations, and I have highlighted the three main areas, offering several places to ski in each. Most of the mountains have a resort or inn. Many New Englanders make day trips to some of these spectacular, fun-filled winter destinations, but if you are coming from far away or want to stay more than a day, all the ski areas offer easy-to-access information about short- and long-term rentals of condos, townhouses, and homes near the mountains. New England skiing is known for more challenging weather. The temperatures get well below freezing most of the winter, the air can be damp, and the wind can whistle right through you, making it feel even colder than it is. That said, New England natives are some of the most rugged and hardiest skiers, so take the climate as a challenge rather than a turnoff.

New Hampshire

New Hampshire offers family skiers great prices, intimate ski areas, and wonderful, kid-friendly mountains. Check out these two mountain resorts.

• *Loon Mountain, Lincoln*—Nestled in the White Mountains, Loon Mountain is a quick two-hour drive from Boston, and its small size makes it perfect for beginning and intermediate skiers. The many slopes offer a variety of ski experiences, from bumps, to glades, to steeps. You and your kids can test yourselves on Loon's signature terrain park and superpipe. Loon also offers well-run children's teaching facilities and programs, including Discovery Camp, for ages seven through twelve; Kinder Bear, for ages four through six; and P.K. Boos, for three-year-olds; as well as kids' camp specials. There is plenty of on-mountain lodging, as well as three nearby choices, Comfort Inn & Suites, the family-owned Woodward's Resort, and the InnSeason Resort, a hotel/condominium complex suitable for every taste and budget. Contact www.loonmtn.com.

• *Ragged Mountain Resort, Danbury*—Ragged Mountain, in the "new Blue Hills," is an affordable, accessible ski destination with a full-service resort and spa. It offers the most inexpensive big-mountain skiing and snowboarding experiences in New England, with more than two hundred acres of trails, 98 percent state-of-the-art snowmaking coverage, nine lifts, and two New England colonial–style lodges that provide all the amenities a family could need. It is also becoming one of the premier teaching facilities in New England geared toward young skiers. In a unique program for kids two and a half through four, your "ski puppies" can get started on skis. It also offers a huge "ski-wee" facility for slightly older and more experienced small skiers. One other nice note—the fastest-growing resort in the area recently added lights for night skiing. The "welcome to snow" package is the ideal learning environment, with more than fifty trails and a high-speed, six-passenger chairlift. Contact www.newbluehills.com.

Maine

Most people don't think of Maine as ski country, but this vast state contains some truly spectacular ski areas and some New Englanders' family favorites.

• *Sugarloaf*—Sugarloaf is Maine's largest single ski mountain. It features extensive terrain for all abilities and an award-winning slope-side village brimming with activities, fabulous restaurants, shops, and resort lodging from hotels, to inns, to condominiums. With great snowmaking abilities, Sugarloaf is a laid-back, family-friendly ski destination. Contact www.sugarloaf.com for more information.

• *Sunday River*—Sunday River contains eight interconnected mountain peaks, which give visitors terrific options for skiing and boarding. Make sure you get to the North Peak Lodge for an outdoor lunch on its deck overlooking the slopes. There is plenty for your family to enjoy off-mountain, too. The White Cap Fun Center offers tubing, ice skating, dining, and more. You can explore the Maine woods on snowshoes, snowmobiles, or cross-country skis. Or, if you'd prefer fun of the indoor variety, nearby Bethel offers an indoor climbing wall, laser tag, a movie theater, and shopping. When it's time to eat, you'll have your choice of more than twenty restaurants and ten bars, including a microbrewery. It's also very easy to travel between the mountain and the town, with a free shuttle system. Your lodging options are also great, with more than seven hundred condominiums, a comfortable inn, and two hotels—all slope-side. Contact www.sundayriver.com.

Northern Vermont

• **Smuggler's Notch**—This mountain is known for its commitment to families and skiing, and many return year after year, eventually buying condos right on the mountain. This family-friendly environment is perfect for the avid skiing family. Smuggs, as it refers to itself, is all about family fun and adventure. The main resort offers an indoor heated pool and hot tubs, outdoor natural ice skating rink, a cross-country and snowshoe adventure center, and a unique indoor playland called the FunZone Family Entertainment and Recreation Center. The FunZone offers music and activities, including an obstacle course, a jousting room, and a bouncy house. Kids can also play miniature golf or shoot hoops in the basketball corner. Contact www.smuggs.com for more information.

Central Vermont

• **Killington**—Killington is the largest winter sports resort in the East. It offers five base lodges from which to ski, and each lodge offers skiers and boarders different options, depending on your interests and ski level. Killington is known for its well-defined array of kids' programs, including specific programs for kids ages two and three, four through six, seven through twelve, and thirteen through seventeen. The

Friendly Penguin Day Care, for kids six weeks to six years, is a state-licensed and fully equipped facility providing toys and games in a nurturing environment. Families can stay at either the Killington Resort Villages or the Killington Grand Resort Hotel. Contact www.killington.com for more information.

• ***Okemo Mountain, Ludlow***—Many locals do day trips at Okemo, one of the medium-size mountains in Vermont. Offering extensive program for kids of all ages and skill levels, as well as competition and clinics for adults, Okemo is a well-rounded ski area with plenty of on-mountain lodging and other affordable options nearby. For further information contact www.okemo.com.

Southern Vermont

• ***Bromley***—Voted number one for family ski programs in *Ski* magazine, Bromley is a terrific, laid-back mountain—perfect for families. Its centrally located base lodge makes it easy for families to meet and gather. Featuring a huge fieldstone fireplace, this classic lodge has all the charm of an old-fashioned ski resort. Nervous about letting the kids go on their own? You can keep in touch with Motorola radios, available in the rental center. Bromley is just six miles east of historic Manchester and offers a huge array of lodging options on-mountain, off-mountain, and for every budget. Contact www.bromley.com for further information.

• ***Stratton Mountain***—Also near Manchester, Stratton is both a mountain and a village, with great dining, sports center activities, and of course, great skiing and boarding. Although Stratton is known for its range of lodging options, including spacious condominiums, its primary draw is big-mountain skiing and snowboarding. Stratton boasts number-one terrain parks, a family-friendly learning park, and a slope-side village lined with shops and restaurants (including family fare and takeout), fun events and activities, plus child care for ages six weeks and older, full-day ski and snowboard instruction for ages four and up. Contact www.stratton.com for more information.

These mountains are great for young families because they offer strong children's programs and on-mountain lodging, as well as nearby condo rentals, B&Bs, and inns. For your complete guide to skiing in Vermont, including a map of the state detailing each mountain's location, contact www.skivermont.com.

Once in a Lifetime Winter Trip:

Stowe, Vermont

Located in northern Vermont, Stowe is the quintessential ski destination. As part of the mighty Mt. Mansfield, it offers visitors exceptional skiing, boarding, and other winter sport options, plus your choice of top-rated resorts and inns at which to stay and both casual and fine dining experiences for the entire family to enjoy. The historic village features a charming assortment of lodging, antiques, galleries, and award-winning cuisine. Beautiful summers and spectacular fall foliage make Stowe a resort destination for any season, but it's wintertime when most people enjoy this spectacular region most. Activities, including cross-country skiing, sleigh riding, and skating, and full-service spa treatments are plentiful and offered at most of the inns and resorts. Located forty-five minutes from Lake Champlain, Stowe offers a wonderful way to see and experience Vermont. If you want to treat your family to a memorable winter vacation, Stowe, Vermont, should be your destination! Here are the featured resorts:

• **Stoweflake Mountain Resort and Spa**—A family-owned and operated full-service resort, the Stoweflake offers pampering amenities (such as fine dining and a full-service spa), exceptional service, and virtually unlimited activities—both indoor and outdoor. It is ideally located between Stowe Village and the majestic Mt. Mansfield. It's just four miles from the ski area and thirty-five miles from Burlington International Airport.

- ***Topnotch at Stowe Resort and Spa***—Rated among the best places to stay in the world by *Condé Nast Traveler* and located on 120 acres, Topnotch is four miles from the historic Stowe Village and five minutes from the ski slopes. It offers two restaurants on the premises, with spectacular mountain views or cozy fireside dining, that specialize in global continental spa cuisine. Make sure you check in to Topnotch's spa packages, as well. If tennis is your game, bring your racquet—the indoor tennis program is rated number one in New England by *Tennis* magazine. Contact www.topnotchresort.com for more information.

- ***Trapp Family Lodge***—Yes, the family immortalized in *The Sound of Music* came to Vermont after leaving Austria and opened this lodge. The Trapp Family Lodge, still family owned, is absolutely picturesque, with miles and miles of cross-country trails that take you through woods, open space, and even to the chapel where Maria used to say her prayers! Your kids will have a ball at the Mountain Kids Club, which organizes and supervises activities such as cross-country skiing, family sledding, snowshoeing, snowman building competitions, and snow fort building. This mountain lodge hotel offers comfortable accommodation in rooms, suites, and houses. It also includes two restaurants, two outdoor heated pools, four tennis courts, a sports center with indoor pool, and a sauna and exercise room. If you like to downhill, you can ski at Stowe, which is only a few miles away! Contact www.trappfamily.com for more information.

- ***Green Mountain Inn***—This inn was built as a private residence in 1833 and was recently beautifully restored. It offers guests the perfect blend of modern comfort and country elegance, with one hundred antiques-furnished rooms, fireplace suites, Mill House and Depot luxury rooms, and two exquisite village apartments. The newest accommodations are in the Mansfield House, featuring twenty-two exceptional guest rooms and suites. Amenities at the Green Mountain Inn include a cozy library and living room, two acclaimed restaurants, a fully equipped health club, game room, and a year-round outdoor heated swimming pool. The inn is close to skiing, hiking, shopping, and many other area attractions.

Beyond Our Borders

Skiing is popular all around the world. When you and your family are ready to head to distant mountains and experience the thrill of skiing in a foreign land, you may want to consider such magnificent ski areas as Whistler Mountain in Canada's British Columbia; Salzburg, Austria, where the Von Trapp family originated; the superposh Courcheval, France; and the Termas Ski and Spa Resort in Chile—but make sure you go during summer, when South America is having its winter season!

Checklist for Winter Vacations

- ❏ As you research winter resorts, inquire about ski packages.
- ❏ Ask if the resort is located at the mountain, or, if not, how close to the ski mountain it is.
- ❏ Make sure it offers children's lessons and clinics with experienced professionals.
- ❏ Inquire about nonski children's programs, especially if your kids are young.
- ❏ Inquire about other activities available for nonskiers.
- ❏ Decide on equipment. Are you bringing your own, or are you

renting? If renting, inquire about costs, age of equipment, and other necessary information. Sometimes it is cheaper and more convenient to rent at home or from an off-site ski shop.

❏ Ask whether your accommodations have a hot tub, sauna, whirlpool, or pool.

❏ Find out if spa services are available at your resort or at a resort nearby.

❏ Pack all the necessary clothes for outdoor and indoor comfort, and make sure everything still fits.

❏ Pack assorted sources of quiet entertainment, such as books, movies, music, and games for you and your kids to enjoy by the fire.

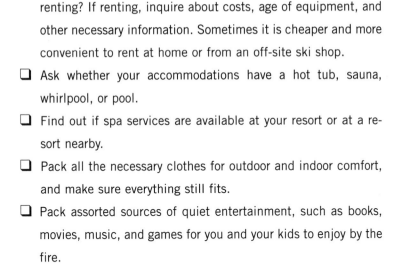

• *Golden Moment Rule #6* •

Take a Hot Bath

*N*ow of course this suggestion comes with tired ski legs in mind. But really all of us could use this advice, no matter what kind of vacation we're on or what the weather outside. The ancients have always known the power of water to calm the body and the mind, so wherever you happen to be, try a good long soak. You deserve it!

A winter vacation can be cozy and warm as you snuggle by a fire, or it can be exhilarating and breathtaking as you ski or board down snow-swept mountains, taking in the cold winter air. But if winter weather is not what you have in mind for a family vacation, let's take a look at the luxury you can find at an all-inclusive resort.

. SEVEN .

One for All:
All-Inclusive Resorts

We all relax and enjoy ourselves in different ways, at different paces, and at different levels of intensity. All-inclusive resorts cater to this diversity. For one family, a day of fun and relaxation may be playing beach volleyball and taking rides on the banana boat. Another family may prefer to sit on lounge chairs all day, reading books while basking in the sun. Other families love resorts where they can explore the ocean through scuba diving and snorkeling. The beauty of all-inclusive resorts is that no matter where you are and who you are, you can find the perfect way to relax and have fun. My husband loves to spend vacations at all-inclusive resorts because he knows that once he arrives, he can relax and unwind at his own pace while the kids and I jump right into activities—no one is holding anyone back from enjoying the vacation.

Another of the main reasons so many families are flocking to all-inclusive resorts for vacation is that they can find the most enjoyment for the maximum value. These prepackaged vacations offered by all-inclusive resorts typically include lodging, dining, and a myriad of entertainment riches all in one place. Many all-inclusive resorts are beachfront and located in warm climates, including the Caribbean, the Bahamas, Mexico, Jamaica, and some stateside in Florida. Depending on their ages, your kids can participate in kid club activities, supervised jaunts around the resort, or, if they're still in diapers, be watched over by trusted professionals. Above all, you want to make sure that the resort you choose is geared toward families. I know of one family who arrived on the balmy shores of a Negril resort only to discover themselves walking into a nude wedding party—in one shocking instant, they realized they were not at a family-friendly resort!

All-inclusive resorts vary in terms of price, level of luxury and service, and assortment of activities and entertainment, but all of them offer amenities that include swimming pools, exercise facilities, dining rooms and/or restaurants (often theme-related dining experiences), and other entertainment geared to adults. My best advice: Do your homework and know the resort and its all-inclusive package before booking. As you consider which resort is right for you and your family, always keep in mind your budget, and make sure you ask exactly what is included in the all-inclusive rate. For example, some package deals or all-inclusive resorts may seem at initial glance to be too steep for your budget. However, when you figure that all costs are included, the price may be reasonable. The opposite is also true: Some package deals and all-inclusive resorts post costs exclusive of certain amenities, such as babysitting, alcohol, spa services, and specific activities. Make sure you understand what the comprehensive price includes. Always read the fine print because the too-good-to-be-true all-inclusive vacation may be just that: There may be a cap on how much you can drink, eat, and play. Some resorts are located in secluded areas of otherwise busy islands. You may want to inquire if there are any safety issues on- or off-site, or whether the resort itself is walled off, which may speak for itself. The magic of an all-inclusive resort is that there should be no surprises, no hidden costs, and everyone is completely on vacation!

Since most all-inclusive resorts involve getting there by air, you may want to consider some tips for saving money in other areas:

• Seek out travel agents who specialize in all-inclusive vacation travel, including packagers such as VacationOutlet.com, vacationstogo.com, sunvacations.org, and all-inclusives.com, a few of many.

• Some all-inclusive resorts own their own airlines and can offer better deals on air travel. For instance, Air Jamaica and Sandals are owned by the same company. When you book directly through them (either one), you will get the best all-inclusive price. American Airlines Vacations also offers great package deals that include air travel and hotel stays at all-inclusive resorts.

• If you have heard about a resort from word of mouth, contact it directly and ask for a vacation package.

• Travel search engines such as Travelocity, Expedia, Orbitz, and Cheap Tickets all offer vacation packages.

It's always a good idea to comparison shop and know the other offers out there. You need to feel confident that your all-inclusive package includes direct air travel to the resort destination, transport from the airport to the resort, and hotel/resort accommodations.

Resort Destinations

Many of the all-inclusive resorts are parts of larger chains that have resorts in several locations, and some chains cater to families and kids better than others. As you begin to consider where you want to go and what type of resort you think you might enjoy, consider how much they offer children. Also, all of the chains have Web sites that can link you to each of their individual locations, so researching is a much easier task than you might think. Here I highlight a representative sampling of all-inclusive resorts.

Beaches Resorts

The Beaches chain (part of the Sandals company) of all-inclusive resorts has four prime locations in the Caribbean—Negril, Jamaica, Boscobel, and Turks and Caicos. As guaranteed all-inclusives, the Beaches resorts are known for their luxurious accommodations, impeccable service, and high-end locations. You truly get what you pay for. Their all-inclusive promise includes such standard features as beer, wine, premium liquor, and tipping, but it's the complete range of activities and amenities that make a Beaches resort a first-class family destination. In their all-inclusive price they include water sports, scuba diving, golf (in Jamaica), pools and whirlpools, spa services, fitness centers, and their renowned Kid Kamps. These well-run kids' centers offer separate programs for various age groups (toddlers, tweeners, and teens), and the activities are age appropriate and entertaining. For very young kids, Beaches offers a professionally trained nursery staffed by its "ultra nannies," who are highly trained by university child developmental specialists. In their capable hands, babies are fed, changed, and rocked gently to sleep. Beaches also provides strollers, cribs, high chairs, and more, so you don't have to worry about lugging all that baby equipment with you. One-on-one babysitting is also available, day and night, at an additional cost. And there's a nurse on property twenty-four hours a day. Check out their Web site for further information: www.beaches.com.

Club Med Family Vacations

A longtime leader in the all-inclusive vacation, Club Med knows how to have fun and keep everyone active! Its resorts and packages are definitely geared toward active families, though their style is a bit less luxurious than that of the Beaches resorts. Put it this way: If you're into ultra comfort, bring your own down pillow. Even without the luxurious bells and whistles, my family has had fabulous vacations at a number of Club Med sites. On a visit to their Paradise Island location in the Bahamas, Gabby, then nine years old, hung out the entire week with a young French girl who spoke not a word of English—and Gabby didn't speak a word of French! Many of the people who work at Club Meds are young Europeans taking some time off from real life back home. So you get a bit of cultural exposure as well as a fabulous vacation.

With so-called Villages all over the world, a number of Club Med destinations are located in the United States proper, as well as Mexico and the Caribbean. Here is a brief rundown on a few of the individual resorts that specialize in serving families:

Crested Butte, Colorado

This is one of very few family winter vacation destinations set up as an all-inclusive. It offers ski lessons, snowboarding lessons, free all-day passes, as well as other outdoor activities, though some, like horseback riding and dogsledding, are at an extra cost.

Sandpiper, Port St. Lucie, Florida

This resort offers a fun and relaxing vacation for the whole family. The village is perfect for golf and tennis lovers and offers families specialty children programs: Baby Club Med (4–23 months), Petit Club Med (2–3 years), Mini Club Med (4–10 years), and Junior Club Med (11–13 years and teenagers during holidays). Located on the sparkling St. Lucie River, it is a pristine little village all on its own. Whether you crave nine iron or net action, this glorious four-hundred-acre country club in the heart of the Florida's Treasure Coast appeals most to families who enjoy tennis, golf, and pool hopping, as there is no beach. As usual, this Club Med is an all-inclusive that includes a full open bar and all-day dining. Known for its gourmet kitchens, Club Med also offers endless buffets and a variety of dining options, from elegant sit-down meals to snacks—all day long!

Caravelle, Guadeloupe

This Club Med is located on one of the islands that make up the archipelago of Guadeloupe, the center of the Caribbean's Creole culture, showing its ties to both French and African influences. Families can find a relaxed yet festive atmosphere while enjoying the Creole-inspired food, the soft golden beaches, and the exotic rain forest nearby. So whether you want to lie back and relax or go exploring, Caravelle offers options for everyone.

Punta Cana, Dominican Republic

Here, children are kings, and their castle is an oceanfront Mini Club Med, complete with its own pool, tennis court, and playground. The whole family can relax on the longest hotel beach on the island and play in the surf, which is perfect for sailing and snorkeling. This is a prime location, and a charming resort—your worries will blow away with the warm Caribbean breeze. More treasures await beyond this magnificent seventy-four-acre village—from tropical rain forests and river cruises to the charm of Santo Domingo, the oldest city in the New World.

For further information about Club Med vacations, visit www. clubmed.com.

Super Clubs

The Super Clubs resort chain owns some of the Caribbean's prime and most lush beachfront property. With resorts in Nassau and the Bahamas, Jamaica, the U.S. Virgin Islands, and the Dominican Republic, Super Clubs all offer oceanfront settings, elegantly manicured grounds, and many water sports—but not all of them are geared toward families. Remember the nude wedding? So as you begin your search (www.superclubs.com) make sure you select only those resorts that fit your needs. The Breezes line is part of the Super Club chain but is moderate in cost and offers a lot of activities, entertainment, and other amenities to families. It guarantees that children will enjoy their program or your money will be refunded!

Breezes, Curaçao

This resort is the first Super Club resort in the southern Caribbean. The Dutch roots of this island add a bit of cultural flavor to this beautiful spot. Only a ninety-minute flight from Montego Bay, Curaçao is located off the coast of Venezuela and is a diver's paradise. The resort offers spacious, charming rooms and suites, great dining options, and Camp Breezes for kids. Kids will also enjoy the Undersea National Park and entertaining Sea Aquarium, just outside the resort. And while the kids are enjoying themselves, the parents can have their own fun at the on-site casino and spa.

Sauipe, Brazil

The first and only Super-Inclusive resort in all of South America, this Breezes resort is located on the north coast of the state of Bahia, Brazil, on the coast of the Atlantic Ocean. You and your family can enjoy a variety of land and water sports, six theme restaurants to suit every appetite, and deluxe rooms and suites. This resort also offers Camp Breezes, a fully supervised kids program. As an added incentive for bringing your entire family, at Sauipe kids fourteen and under stay, play, and eat FREE!

Starfish Trelawny, Jamaica

The Starfish is a beautiful oceanfront resort nestled into one of Jamaica's beaches. Its accommodations are charming, with private balconies or porches, and the staff is known to be friendly and very welcoming. Kids will go crazy over the five pools—one with a waterslide, one for activities, and one exclusively for toddlers. Parents will enjoy private sundecks and cabanas, an open-air massage on the resort's private island, the casino, and other spa services. Every Friday night the resort throws circus parties. And the disco will keep kids entertained for hours. If you are itching for a little culture, you can explore the local arts and crafts at the nearby Bamboo Village. The resort's all-inclusive plan includes the typical lodging, meals, fitness center, most recreation facilities, golf, airport transfers, taxes, and gratuities. It does not include certain meals, such as lobster and shrimp, motorized water sports, flying trapeze and circus workshop, beauty services, rock climbing tower, Internet access, children's club, and babysitting, as well as other amenities.

For further information about assorted Breezes vacation packages, visit www.breezes.com.

Palace Resorts

Karmina Palace, Manzanillo, Mexico

This all-inclusive resort set on Mexico's Riviera, along the Costa Alegre below Puerto Vallarta, is absolutely beautiful. A 324-suite hotel, it offers spacious suites, family-oriented entertainment, and many activities, including horseback riding through the jungle, scuba diving, snorkeling, and deep-sea fishing, as well as a full-service spa and game room. The hotel also offers twenty-four-hour room service and several dining options. It's kids' club offers supervised activities for kids age six and older. My son considers this "a very cool all-inclusive."

The five other Palace Resorts, all in Mexico, include Aventura Spa Palace, a six-star resort; Xpu-Ha Palace, a four-star resort in the Mayan Riviera; and Moon Palace, Beach Palace, and Sun Palace, all in Cancún in the Yucatán province of Mexico. They often offer special discounts for families during summer, and each year they add more to their kids' programs. For further information, contact www.palaceresorts.com.

Viva Wyndham

Viva Wyndham is the less expensive line of Wyndham resorts, located in tropical settings in the Dominican Republic, the Bahamas, and Mexico, and is especially family-friendly. Many of the resorts offer family suites, furnished with colorful bunk beds, art tables, and child-size chairs. These eight resorts offer fabulous family incentives, such as kids' stay, play, and eat for free or for a nominal fee. All the resorts offer organized kids' clubs and babysitting, off-site excursions, Caribbean dance classes, and daily activities that include water sports, sailing, beach and pool volleyball, and archery. Parents will find their pleasure, too. Yoga and meditation, local cooking classes, theater, casino action, and both elegant and casual dining options are available.

The Dominican Republic

There are five Viva Wyndham resorts here:

• ***Dominicus Beach*** hosts three pools and four restaurants, lighted tennis courts for nighttime play, as well as basketball and a soccer field. This quaint Caribbean setting makes for a low-key and relaxed feel.

• ***Dominicus Palace*** has one pool and seven restaurants. Next door to Dominicus Beach, the Palace's colonial-style buildings give this resort a more elegant flair.

• ***Tangerine*** has superior ocean views, and many of its rooms have balconies from which to view the sea.

• ***Samaná,*** with a full-service spa and sauna and a wealth of outdoor activities, features a freshwater pool with kids' area, beach bar, snack bar/pizzeria, and three restaurants.

• ***Playa Dorada,*** the only Viva Wyndham resort not located right on the beach, is a brand-new facility. It offers a Trent B. Jones–designed eighteen-hole golf course, lush mountains as its backdrop, full spa services, and a mall within the resort itself.

Grand Bahama Island

• ***Viva Wyndham Fortuna*** is on the Bahama Islands. Quieter than Nassau, Grand Bahama Island offers families the perfect secluded spot to vacation. This resort emphasizes lots of activities, sports, and water action.

The Mexican Riviera

Here you will find two Viva Wyndham resorts.

• ***The Azteca,*** the smaller of the two, is located on the pristine island of Playa del Carmen.

• **The Maya,** which has four hundred rooms, is situated on the beach and close to fascinating Mayan ruins of Chichen Itza and Tulum.

For more information about Viva Wyndham all-inclusive resorts, contact www.wyndham.com.

Once in a Lifetime All-Inclusive:

The Magical World of Disney, Lake Buena Vista, Florida

The longtime king of the all-inclusive vacation is Walt Disney himself. No one understands children better than the people who design and run the Disney all-inclusive packages, so my choice for a "once in a lifetime" trip in this vacation category has to be a family trip to Walt Disney World. (You will read all about their truly magical cruises in Chapter 8!)

A rite of passage for kids and adults alike, Disney World includes a vast myriad of theme parks, wildlife-related sites, water parks, and live entertainment, shows, and movies, as well as a full range of accommodations and dining options. On its forty-seven square miles of terrain, six unique but interconnected sites await your visit: the Magic Kingdom, Epcot, Disney-MGM Studios, Disney's Animal Kingdom, Downtown Disney, and a sports complex. Each of these areas offers its own thematic dining experiences, rides for kids and adults of all ages (most of the rides have height restrictions), and live entertainment, including parades, circuslike shows, and much, much more.

How to Design Your Visit

If the Walt Disney World Resort is your destination of choice, there are many ways you can plan your vacation. Indeed, when you go to its Web site (www.disneyworld.com), it will lead you through an interactive vacation-planner, so you can better decide on how you want to spend your time and money. Disney's standard vacation package is called the Dream Maker and includes on-site lodging and Park Hopper passes. Packages range in price based on length of stay, age of children, and resort choice. And if you wish, Disney can also arrange your flight, but you might not get the best deal. However, some airlines do offer packages that include airfare, Disney World Resort accommodations, and theme park admissions.

Disney has also come up with a new way to customize your vacation plan called Magic Your Way, based on your length of stay, level of accommodations, dining options, and access to the theme parks. Magic Your Way vacation packages are fabulously flexible, so you can put together your dream vacation on the budget you want. They include:

- Disney resort stay—Select your preferred Disney resort category: value, moderate, or deluxe.

- Magic Your Way Base Ticket—Visit one theme park a day each day of your trip.

- Park Hopper Pass—Unlimited admission to all four parks and water parks.

- Extra Magic Hours—Extra time in the theme parks for Disney resort guests lets you enjoy select attractions at a more leisurely pace.

- Guest transportation—Zip around on complimentary and convenient transportation that runs continuously throughout the day.

- Dining option—Includes one table service meal, one counter service meal, and one snack for each person every day of your visit.

Where to Stay

Although you can stay outside Disney World itself, it is generally more enjoyable to stay on-site, and it's when you stay within the World that your visit truly becomes an all-inclusive-style vacation. Many (I would say most) families decide to stay on-site because of the proximity to all the venues, the ease of transportation (many resorts offer monorail, ferry, and trolley service from the resort to the various theme parks), and the ability to package their entire vacation—airfare, accommodations, and entrance into the theme parks—into one price. The people at Disney want to make you happy, and they want you to return. If you stay at one of the hotels within Disney World itself, it provides another service called Magical Express. You contact Disney services several weeks before your trip to give them your flight information. It will send you bright yellow luggage tags to put on your suitcases. When you arrive at the Orlando Airport, Disney arranges to have your luggage transferred to your hotel, and you are free to go either right to your hotel or to a theme park.

Some families who want a bit of distance between themselves and the World prefer to stay off-site; if this is the case for you, all of the major chain hotels and motels, as well as some rental condos, are available. You may also find lower prices for accommodations off-site. You can research these options through the usual avenues and see page 21 for specific suggestions.

Within Disney itself, there are thirty-two places to stay at a variety of prices—from Disney campsites to value, moderate, and deluxe resorts. Each of the eight parks offers its own selection of accommodations in the three price-point categories, which Disney defines the following way:

A Value Category Resort Offers	A Moderate Category Resort Offers	A Deluxe Category Resort Offers
Themed pools	Pools with slides	Elaborately themed pools
Food courts	Full-service dining	World-class restaurants
Pizza delivery	Pizza delivery	Room service
Maximum four guests per room	Marina Watercraft rentals	Marina watercraft rentals
	Room service	Whirlpools
	Whirlpools	Babysitting
	Maximum five guests per room	Valet parking
		Character breakfasts
		Concierge available
		Fitness center/spa
		Maximum five guests per room

For more specific information about the hotels and their locations, services, and rates, contact www.disneyworld.com.

When to Go

My family keeps returning to Disney World because of its endless supply of entertainment, relaxation, and surprises. Because of our repeat visits, we have learned a few tricks of the trade when it comes to timing Disney World vacations:

- Avoid holidays; the resorts get very busy and overcrowded.

- Avoid summer—especially if you are traveling with very young children or older adults. Summer in Orlando is hotter than hot, and kids and older adults will tire easily. Also, the crowds are voluminous.

- Arrive early in the day, take a break in the middle of the day, and return in the evening. You need to rest, and there is an ebb and flow

> ## REMEMBER NOT TO OVERDO IT!
>
> Nowhere is it more mandatory than at Disney World to remember not to try to do too much! You must schedule downtime, which is why staying on-site is often a good idea. Kids and adults can rest, nap, or hang out by the pool and zip back to the park when ready.

to the park, with a big rush smack in the middle of the day. If you arrive early, spend a few hours enjoying yourselves, and then take a break back at your hotel when the crowds peak. You will be able to return when the crowds thin out and your energy has returned.

- If you're staying on-site, four days is a good amount of time to experience the world of Disney.

Your Miniguide to Theme Parks

A guide to Disney's four theme parks and two water parks would take pages and pages. Instead, I have highlighted my top three favorite venues at each park. In some cases, I have noted if certain rides are more suitable for younger or older kids.

Magic Kingdom

The Magic Kingdom opened in 1971 and is the oldest of the Disney theme parks. At its center is Cinderella's majestic castle to welcome your family. Within the Magic Kingdom, all of your children's favorite Disney characters come to life. The Magic Kingdom is divided into seven themed lands—Main Street, U.S.A.; Adventureland; Frontierland; Liberty Square; Fantasyland; Mickey's Toontown; and Tomorrowland. Although this park is geared more to younger kids, everyone can find something to do that will bring a smile.

For older kids: Space Mountain, Pirates of the Caribbean, Buzz Lightyear's Space Ranger Spin.

For younger kids: It's a Small World, Peter Pan's Flight, the parades.

Epcot

At the entrance to Epcot looms an enthralling silver sphere, giving visitors an immediate sense of the vastness of the universe in which we live. Epcot, which opened in 1982, invites you to discover intimate encounters with outer space and the richness of the world. Kids and families will experience not only a mission to outer space but also the different cultures found around the world. You can visit various nation villages, including France, Morocco, Italy, Japan, and Mexico, among others.

My top five recommendations for Epcot: Spaceship Earth; Mission: Space; Soarin'; Illuminations; and Honey, I Shrunk the Audience.

Disney-MGM Studios

This theme park, which opened in 1988, is a working film, TV, and radio studio, meant to bring Hollywood to life. With a vast array of films to watch, movie and TV sets to visit, and rides to test out, you and your kids will get lost going Hollywood!

My top three recommendations for Disney-MGM: Indiana Jones Epic Stunt Spectacular; the Twilight Zone Tower of Terror (for older kids); and Playhouse Disney Live on Stage (for younger kids).

Animal Kingdom

The Animal Kingdom is all about bringing the wilderness up close. You and your family will come face-to-face with giraffes, tigers, and rhinos.

You can learn about dinosaurs and tour jungles, forests, and a vast savannah.

My top three recommendations for Animal Kingdom: Kilimanjaro Safaris; Kali River Rapids; and the Gorilla Falls Exploration Trail. A note: It's always best to visit an animal venue in the morning, when the animals are most alert. Afternoon visitors may find the animals asleep!

Blizzard Beach and Typhoon Lagoon

Disney World contains two water parks, Blizzard Beach and Typhoon Lagoon. Kids and adults can body surf, go tubing, and ride roaring rapids. Blizzard Beach has the country's tallest waterslide at 120 feet, and Typhoon Lagoon has a surf pool where you can hop on a board and take to the waves.

My top three recommendations at Blizzard Beach: Slush Gusher (for older kids); Teamboat Springs (for the family); and Tike's Peak (for the little ones).

My top three picks at Typhoon Lagoon: Humunga Kowabunga; Mayday Falls; and the Surf Pool.

Note: Water parks are geared toward older kids, and remember to bring towels and dry clothes!

Downtown Disney

Most of the entertainment venues and evening performances are located in this area of Disney World. The Marketplace is a waterside shopping village with the largest showcase of Disney character merchandise in the world. The west side also contains dining and entertainment, including the fantastic Cirque du Soleil. Disney knows kids, but it also knows adults. Pleasure Island, a six-acre nightclub theme park, features eight nightclubs, plus shops and restaurants. Many character dining experiences and parades take place in Downtown Disney.

My top three suggestions for Downtown Disney: Cirque du Soleil (which requires advance reservations and tickets); character breakfasts (which also have to be arranged in advance); and the Disney Quest.

Where to Eat

Great dining experiences are found all over Disney World, and food is in no short supply. Most of the restaurants offer a family-friendly atmosphere and children's menu, with a wide range of types of food available. A few restaurants offer fine dining, which Disney refers to as Signature Dining.

If you decide to buy the Magic Your Way package, it offers a Dining Plan option, which includes one table service meal, one counter service meal, and one snack for each person every day of your visit. You can use your Key to the World at more than one hundred selected restaurants. Plus, if you would like to eat at a more elegant restaurant, you can exchange two table service meals for one Signature meal. If you want to participate in a Character Dining experience, such as Cinderella's Table, then you can exchange two table service meals for one Character Dining experience. (A full guide to how and where to use the Dining Plan can be downloaded from the Disney World Web site.

As you begin to plan what you want to do, consider where restaurants are located in relation to the rides or venues you'll be visiting. If you want either to dine at a Signature restaurant or to participate in a Character Dining experience, advance reservations are strongly recommended. Reservations can be made up to ninety days in advance and may be arranged with the concierge or guest services at your Disney Resort hotel or by calling 407-939-3463.

Dining at Walt Disney World runs from fast food to fancy. My personal suggestion is to take a break from the parks and eat a late lunch at your hotel so everyone can relax a bit. All the hotels at Disney offer great dining experiences, and you don't have to be a guest at any particular hotel to enjoy the many options, including burgers, seafood, Italian, and southern classic. In the parks, the best dining includes:

Magic Kingdom

- Cinderella's Royal Table and Crystal Palace—both offer Character Dining experiences in which Disney characters entertain, visit tables, and talk to guests
- Cosmic Ray's Starlight Café—for great fast food
- Plaza Restaurant and Tony's Town Square Café

Epcot

- San Angel Inn in Mexico—for fabulous Mexican food
- Bistro de Paris in France—where you feel as if you're sitting in a café in Paris
- Tangieriene Café in Morocco—for fast food options
- Le Cellier Steakhouse—one of my favorites

Disney-MGM Studios

- Hollywood Brown Derby—named and themed after the famous restaurant in L.A.
- 50s Prime Time Café—fun for kids who love eating while watching TV
- Sci-Fi Dine-In Theater Restaurant—another fun one for kids, where they sit in cars and can pretend they're at a drive-in

Animal Kingdom

- Rainforest Café—wide menu set in a jungle atmosphere
- Tusker House—for fast food
- Chakarandi Chicken Shop—in the Asia section of the park

Downtown Disney

- Rainforest Café (a different one)—animals surround you as you eat!
- Bongos Cuban Café—if you like a little spice with your rice and beans
- Wolfgang Puck Café—great pizza and sushi

DISNEY'S VERO BEACH RESORT, VERO BEACH, FLORIDA

*I*f you can't quite handle the thought of a full-blown Disney vacation, a better option is to visit one of Disney's smaller, more manageable resorts. Vero Beach harkens back to the days of an elegant 1900s beach resort. The resort sits on seventy-one acres of beach and parkland, and guests stay in the main building or in various pastel-colored cottages. As you'd expect from Disney, there are plenty of kids' programs, featuring canoeing, scavenger hunts, and campfire tales, and some teen-related activities, as well. Many parents combine a stay here with a visit to Walt Disney World, which is just two hours away. Contact www.disneyworld.com or call 800-500-3990.

Checklist for All-Inclusive Vacations

All-inclusive can mean different things to different people. It's very important that you do your homework and make sure you know what is included in your fee. Here is a sampling of questions to guide you:

- ❑ Is tipping included?
- ❑ Is there any charge for alcoholic beverages?
- ❑ At what age can children participate in activities and programs?

❑ Is babysitting offered for babies and toddlers?

❑ Are the babysitters or caregivers licensed and/or trained, and given background checks?

❑ What kinds of activities do you offer children of various age groups?

❑ What is the adult-to-child ratio in supervised activities?

❑ Are there activities that kids and adults can do together?

❑ Are all meals included in the global fee?

❑ Are all recreational activities included?

❑ Is there a nurse and/or doctor available on the premises?

❑ Are there any excursions offered off-site?

❑ Are baby supplies such as diapers, cribs, and strollers, available, or do we need to bring our own?

Once you have visited an all-inclusive resort, many of these inquiries will become second nature. But on your first or second trip, you want to make sure you know what you are in for.

This listing of all-inclusive destinations is by no means complete. As you begin to research the options, use those described here as a measure of what you want—or don't want. Also, consider another way to experience the all-inclusive vacation: by sea.

• **Golden Moment Rule #7** •

Take a Day Off

*E*ven on vacation, people need a day off. When vacationing at all-inclusive resorts, it's easy to go overboard—on eating, drinking, and even doing activities. Take a day off and do nothing! There's something about having nowhere to go, nothing to do, and a whole day of lounging to make you relax completely. The key is not to plan anything, except perhaps a nap. When you plan nothing for a day, you give yourself much-needed downtime.

. EIGHT .

Smooth Sailing: Family Cruises

No matter how many times we've experienced it, the wonderful feeling of pulling out of port and setting sail on a ship captures the essence of being on vacation. Excitement is in the air, people are ready to relax, and everyone is giddy with anticipation of a marvelous time. We celebrated my father's sixtieth birthday a few years ago with a big extended-family sailing. I will never forget the look of pure happiness on my dad's face as we left the port. The steel drums were playing, people were dancing, and he was surrounded by those who mattered the most in his life.

In the past many people associated cruises with the luxury liners that only the Rockefellers could afford, but now every family, on every budget, can find a cruise to suit its needs. If you and your family have never before considered a cruise, now is the time. Since there are so many cruise lines, ships, and ports of call, prices have come down, making cruises more popular than ever. Today more cruises sail from American ports than ever before. They offer all styles of vacations, accommodations, dining experiences, and activities, some more family-friendly than others.

When planning a cruise, obvious factors to take into consideration are your budget, length of the cruise, departure city, and ports of call. Other factors that may help you decide which cruise is right for your family is the level of formality on board, the activities offered, and the available amenities.

Why Take a Cruise?

Cruising is a great way to travel, especially with a family. Cruises are so easy! You simply check your luggage in at the airport and it ends up in your stateroom. You unpack just once but get to experience several different destinations. The stress and planning around mealtime is eliminated and the kids have plenty of structured activities to participate in, which means that Mom and Dad actually get a vacation, too!

Most cruises have at least one heated pool, some casino options, lots of games and activities for kids and adults, spa services, and spacious sundecks. And while each ship's specific accommodations are different, every ship offers cabins or staterooms on the interior (without a balcony, window, or view of the ocean) or exterior (which has at least a view of the ocean). Anyone prone to motion sickness may want to consider an exterior cabin, as some people experience more motion when inside. And though a window does enhance your view, it will also enhance your bill. Cabins and rooms can vary in size, but most include a private bath, telephone, and television. Depending on the size and makeup of your family, you may need more than one room, adjoining rooms, or a suite.

As I said, cruises really are one of my family's favorite ways to travel. They are appropriate for people of all ages, but the key is to match your vacation expectation with the offerings of each cruise line. Every week new ships are introduced that are bigger and faster, but for a family vacation, it is important to understand what is provided on each ship to keep the kids and grown-ups happy. Here is a sampling of various cruise lines and what they offer.

Disney Cruise Lines

The Disney Cruise Line offers the very best children's activities at sea. The *Disney Magic* and *Disney Wonder* sail three-, four-, and seven-night cruises out of Port Canaveral in Florida. They provide just enough "Disney" to make the children comfortable without making the parents crazy. Don't worry, you won't be met with the recurring "It's a Small World" song but elegant mahogany banisters and upscale comfort. Disney Cruise Lines pride themselves on what they call the "Disney Difference," and it shows. The programs for kids are structured by age, starting as young as twelve weeks old in the Flounder's Reef Nursery. Preschoolers have their own area, and elementary school kids enjoy their own "lab." Teens are free to come and go to the Common Grounds Teens Only Club. Even my son, who is way too cool to think he can enjoy a Disney vacation, loves this place.

While the kids are busy doing all kinds of fun activities, there are plenty of choices for Mom and Dad. The Rainforest is a spa facility with steam room, sauna, and other treatments for general relaxation. The fitness center on board is loaded with cardio equipment and free weights. An entire deck called Route 66 is devoted to adult fun. You will find a very grown-up piano/martini bar with spectacular views, a comedy night that is just for grown-ups, and lots of dancing in the various nightclubs. Don't worry: Babysitting is available!

With all this adult relaxation, you may even be inspired to spend some quality time with your significant other in the oversize staterooms (complete with a curtain-drawn partition for privacy and two bathroom facilities).

Dining on board a Disney cruise ship is also unique. Each night, guests rotate (along with their servers) through different dining rooms. The Animator's Palate is a visual experience in which the room starts out in black and white and throughout dinner comes to life in living color. Parrot Cay is a Caribbean paradise, with a steel drum band and relaxed atmosphere. Lumiere's and Tritan's are the dress-up, fine dining rooms on board, complete with lobster as a dinner entrée. If you want to have dinner in an adults-only setting, Palo's food and service competes with any big-city eatery.

All in all, Disney Lines are an ideal family cruising choice. From the activities to the extra space in staterooms, they deliver a terrific experience. The prices range from really reasonable for an inside stateroom to quite expensive for top-of-the-line cabins, and these rates change often. As always, I suggest you arm yourself with information and go from there. For more information on a Disney Cruise, visit their Web site at www.disneycruise.com.

Royal Caribbean Cruise Line

Royal Caribbean boasts nineteen ships that sail numerous itineraries throughout countries such as England, Russia, and Greece. While these destinations and ships are nice, I want to focus on the friendliest class of the RCI ships, the Voyager family. These megaships are the *Voyager of the Seas,* the *Explorer of the Seas,* the *Navigator of the Seas,* and the *Adventure of the Seas.* The Voyager ships offer terrific vacations for families who like to keep busy and who are traveling with kids old enough to enjoy activities like ice skating and the climbing wall.

These ships are big. Really big, with capacity to carry more than three thousand passengers. They are so big that they contain a shopping promenade the size of two football fields, complete with an outdoor café where you can sip an espresso and enjoy a pastry. The

Voyager class of ships is terrific for active families. On the top deck, there is a rock climbing wall that towers above the ocean. Guests can tackle the wall as many times as they like during their sailing for no additional charge. Adjacent to the rock wall is an outdoor in-line skating track. Equipment is available for rent with no fee. If ice skating is more your cup of tea, the third deck of these ships is home to an ice skating rink. Ice skates, too, are available for rent on board at no additional charge.

If gaming action gets your heart rate up, you are in luck because there is a casino on every one of these ships. Video poker, slot machines, and card tables are available on which all those over twenty-one can take their chances.

The three-story dining room is simply majestic. Throughout the trip, you are seated at the same table at the same time with the same servers, so if you are someone who likes routine, this is ideal for you. The friendly service and the many food choices on the menu will make you feel like a million bucks.

I've noticed that the younger kids seem to enjoy food that is most familiar and comfortable. If your kids are not up for sitting in the dining room and enjoying a relaxing meal, they can eat at Johnny Rockets with the kids' counselors.

The fitness center and spa are awesome. There is a huge selection of cardio equipment and lots of free weights. Many different exercise classes, such as step aerobics and yoga, are offered throughout each cruise. The spa is a perfect place to unwind. From traditional massages to more exotic wrap treatments, there are services that every guest can be comfortable with. They are a bit pricey, but once you are on vacation, why not splurge a little?

The programming for children is good: Though not terribly creative, it is safe and fun. Teenagers and preteens can come and go from the program, and there really is so much to do that they keep themselves very busy. A prominent new feature is the Adventure Ocean Youth program, which is devoted to opening the minds of young people. Kids can learn about the science of sailing or a new sport such as gagaball. The *Explorer* recently added a state-of-the-art oceanography lab run by the University of Miami.

The seven-night itineraries change depending on which ship you select. Among its over ten different ships, the *Adventure of the Seas* departs from San Juan, Puerto Rico, and sails through the Caribbean, and the *Mariner of the Seas* leaves from Port Canaveral, Florida, and sails to the Bahamas and upper Caribbean. If you are ready for a European cruise, the *Voyager of the Seas* makes several trips from Barcelona, Spain, to ports in France and Italy. For additional information on these cruises, explore the Royal Caribbean Web site at www.royalcaribbean.com.

Norwegian Cruise Line

Norwegian boasts thirteen ships that sail ten different itineraries. The fleet visits more than 140 ports around the world, but Norwegian has a huge commitment to domestic sailing. Cruises leave year-round from Houston, Miami, New York, New Orleans, Honolulu, and Los Angeles. For people who are concerned about traveling out of the country, NCL is the perfect choice to feel safe and secure.

Norwegian has two great big ships—the *Dawn* and the *Star*—each with more than 1,100 guest cabins. Both feature garden villas, simply the best accommodations at sea. They are multiroom, top-of-the-line guest suites with a roof terrace, private Jacuzzi, a living room, and two bedrooms with king-size beds. If you are looking for an elegant albeit pricey experience on a cruise, this is definitely it. Those looking for a more economical sailing can choose other cabins.

In addition to the *Dawn* and the *Star,* NCL built a third ship, the *Sun,* for "freestyle cruising." Most cruise lines offer a structured sailing experience with a scheduled seating time and dining rotation. NCL passengers create their own dining experiences on board by selecting where they want to eat (there are eleven restaurants to pick from on the *Dawn*), what time they would like to dine, and the atmosphere of the venue, from formal to casual. There are even special restaurants designated for families that feature buffets for the kids.

The Kids' Crew program is structured for children ages two through seventeen and caters to the needs of each specific age. The T-Rex Kids' Center is a supervised play area that also includes Flick's Movie Theater with kid-friendly selections, Click's Computer Center, and Doodle's Art Area. Teens have a separate facility that is a fifties diner during the day and a disco just for them at night.

When the kids are involved with other kids, Mom and Dad have time for some fun with plenty of adult-oriented activities. The El Dorado Spa on the *Dawn* has fifteen treatment rooms (one designated for couples!), and the fitness center has plenty of cardio equipment and exercise classes. It boasts the longest indoor lap pool on a cruise ship, as well as special hydrotherapy rooms. If casino action is more your idea of unwinding, these ships offer lots of gaming options, such as roulette, craps, blackjack, and slot machines. You can find places to cut loose and get your groove on or simply unwind in the wine cellar, complete with wine tasting seminars.

As you know, Hawaii is one of my all-time favorite family vacation destinations, and Norwegian Cruise Lines sail two different ships in the Hawaiian Islands, departing from Honolulu (NCL also offers cruise packages that include round-trip airfare to and from Honolulu). I personally love the *Pride of Aloha*. This seven-day Hawaiian cruise gives you the perfect chance to explore the islands of Maui, Kauai, and Hawaii and experience what makes each one of them unique. You are not rushed on and off the ship, as the *Pride of Aloha* stays overnight, allowing you to spend time at each island. Guests can leisurely explore each destination on their own terms and their own budget.

If you are interested in more information about Norwegian Cruise Lines, visit their Web site at www.ncl.com.

Carnival Fun Ships

Carnival has one of the largest fleets of "fun ships" in the world. Its twenty-one ships sail throughout the Caribbean, Hawaii, the Bahamas, and Mexico, as well as to Alaska, Canada, and New England. Carnival also has ships that make transatlantic crossings to Europe, as well as ships that cruise within Europe itself. Indeed, if you and your family are ready to experience foreign travel, taking a cruise to Europe is a wonderful way to get your feet wet.

The latest addition to the line is the *Carnival Valor,* which is 952 feet long, with thirteen different decks, designed with family vacations in mind. It departs from Miami and voyages throughout the eastern and western Caribbean on a seven-day trip. As with most of the Carnival ships, it includes wonderful entertainment for kids and adults alike. With four pools, including a six-foot waterslide, kids will have a ball while parents relax with its first-class spa services, in its casino, and at its live entertainment shows. Kids will be well taken care of when they participate in age-appropriate activities both on the ship and during shore excursions. Some recent shore excursions include swimming with the dolphins, canopy camping adventures, and white-water rafting. If you want guided advice on which trip and ship are right for you and your family, you can use Carnival's vacation planning service or the online Cruise Wizard to help you decide on and design your own cruise.

For more specific information, contact www.carnival.com.

Once in a Lifetime Cruise:

Princess Cruise to Alaska

Taking a cruise to Alaska is quite simply a majestic experience. And though a number of cruise lines now offer Alaskan trips, Princess Cruises is my personal preference for sailing as a family because Princess has partnered with the Junior Ranger and Teen Explorer programs and created top-of-the-line shore excursions. It's these trips into the wilderness that make a vacation so special, though they are definitely the most expensive activities as far as ports of call and cruise lines go. The activities are designed to bring Glacier Bay and the Alaskan wilderness to life for the thousands of children who sail with Princess each summer.

The National Parks Service has worked with the cruise line to develop programming that is fun and entertaining and customized to kids. Naturalists (not the naked kind but the informative kind) are standing by to guide you through all of the wilderness, geography, and wildlife of the region. They can take you—via seaplane—to the edge of a glacier or to remote areas where you will observe black bears catching fish in their natural habitat. Your kids will be thrilled when they pan for gold in streams, catch salmon and bring it back to the ship for the chef to prepare, or kayak off the tip of an iceberg.

Princess offers seven different ships that sail seven-night to ten-night itineraries through some of the most beautiful scenery in the world. On the Voyage of the Glaciers cruise, four of the ships sail between Vancouver, British Columbia, and Whittier, the gateway to Anchorage. These seven-day cruises take you to Juneau and Skagway, made famous by the Klondike Gold Rush, and allow you to see salmon runs in Ketchikan and glory in the glaciers of Glacier Bay. The Inside Passage cruise is designed to explore historic Alaskan towns and cruise the glaciers into Tracy Arm. Two ships, the *Diamond Princess* and *Sap-*

phire Princess, offer seven-day round-trips from Seattle, and a third ship, the *Regal Princess,* sails a ten-day round-trip from San Francisco.

The key to enjoying a successful family sail to Alaska is to manage your parental expectations. While adults may marvel at the majestic beauty, kids may not have the same appreciation. I am convinced that they are affected by the experience and later in life will be grateful to have done this, but don't set yourself up for disappointment by thinking they will immediately share your emotional high. Also, remember that in summer (especially early summer), Alaska stays light late—really late—making it difficult for some kids to adjust their sleep patterns.

When not immersed in the Alaskan environment, kids and adults have plenty to do. Each of the ships sailing the Alaska itinerary has pools, spas, twenty-four-hour dining, casinos, miniature golf, and ded-

MONEY MATTERS

- Bring everything with you that you anticipate needing; medication, film, bottled water, and sunscreen can all be costly on board.

- Buy the drink plans for the kids. When you first board the ship, you may think it is pricey to prepay for unlimited soft drinks, but after ten drinks that never get finished, you will be glad that you did.

- Use the Internet instead of the telephones on the ships. Satellite telephone service is very expensive. For the price of about one call, you can purchase an entire week's worth of Internet use.

- Don't be tempted to buy every photo. Every time I have sailed, professional photographers are waiting to capture each moment that my family experiences, from embarking on the ship, to Formal Night, to disembarking at ports of call. Bring your own camera and save the expense of purchasing the formal portraits.

icated teen and kid space with arts and crafts, movies, video games, and discos. Adults might enjoy the thrill of an authentic art auction or shopping in the upscale boutiques.

Because the scenery is so "once in a lifetime" spectacular, you might want to splurge and get a cabin with a view. However, in case any member of your family needs to sleep in pitch darkness, opting for an elegant interior room is also a comfortable option. You can learn more about the Alaska Princess Cruise at its Web site at www.princesscruises.com.

A Final Note on Cruises

When cruising it's all about avoiding the overs: overpacking, over-scheduling, and overindulging.

- Don't overpack. Space is limited in the cabins, and suitcases simply take up room. You spend most of your time in the same outfit or your bathing suit each day, and there are almost always laundry facilities on board. "Formal Night" can have a broad interpretation, so don't stress out about the wardrobe. Remember that cruising is a relaxed, fun environment, so formal on a ship is not necessarily the same as formal at home.
- Overscheduling on your cruise vacation will leave you finding yourself even more exhausted than before you sailed. You will have so many activities to choose from, and you may feel the need to participate in all of them. Some of my most enjoyable memories have been simply sitting on the deck, soaking up the sun and reading a good book.

Checklist for Cruises

❑ Consider your destination. Do you want a tropical island experience, or are you looking for the hustle and bustle of big-city ports? Do you want to be isolated on a private island owned by the cruise line or cruising through Alaska with nature guides?

❑ Consider duration. How many days at sea do you want? Do you want to be in a different port every day? Do you want to sail for three, four, seven, or ten nights?

❑ Consider dining. Is food an important part of your cruise experience? Do you want to eat in a different restaurant each night? Are you more comfortable dining in the same place with the same servers each night? Do you like to dress up or stay casual?

❑ Consider dollars. What does your budget allow? Do you want an inside or outside stateroom? Do you want to be in luxury accommodations, or is a standard cabin all right?

• *Golden Moment Rule #8* •

Don't Overindulge!

A common association with cruises is the nonstop buffet. Indeed, it is both a pleasure and a peril to be constantly surrounded by delicious, delectable foods to feast on, with sumptuous desserts at each and every meal. After taking almost twenty cruises over the years, I've learned that it's best to start slowly. I also try to remember that the food is not going away, and it's not going to run out, either. A better way to enjoy yourself—and the food—is to eat in moderation. This way you not only get to continue to sample all the foods a cruise has to offer, but you don't end up feeling bloated and guilty for overindulging.

❑ Consider activities. Are there activities that will make every member of your family happy? Is there a structured kids' club? Are there activities that the whole family can enjoy together? Can you find adult time to relax and enjoy your vacation, too?

As parents we pour so much emotion, money, and time into planning our vacations, and we have the fantasy that it will all be smooth sailing 100 percent of the time. Go with the flow, relax, and trust that the kids will appreciate that you took them to see the volcano in Hawaii or that they saw a whale breach in Alaska. Be realistic in managing what your kids can handle, and make sure that there is downtime for you all to recharge your batteries each day.

. NINE .

For the Thrill of It:
The Energy of
Soft Adventures

Vacation is certainly a time for people to be more relaxed than usual. You are out of your normal routine, with new people, in a different place. This environment makes it the perfect time to try something you wouldn't do at home. I've had many vacation adventures during which I catch myself with a huge smile, talking myself through an activity that is particularly challenging. An added bonus is that my kids are impressed that I am willing to try stuff! I have gathered some vacation ideas for what I call "soft adventures" so that you and your family can try something completely new and exciting, too.

Essentially, a soft adventure is all about stepping out of your comfort zone and doing something that gives you a physical, mental, or emotional thrill. We have created a generation of adrenaline junkies, with public middle schools that have rock climbing walls and other ways to mix physical exercise with entertainment. Kids who have grown accustomed to this kind of physical excitement often love the same thrill, rush, and challenge on vacation. As Connie, a mother of two, says, "I am definitely not a risk taker, and neither are my children. But when we tried surfing on a recent vacation to Hawaii, I felt a sense of accomplishment—like I was seventeen again! And watching my kids tackle something as fun and exciting as surfing made them think of themselves differently. When they went back to school, they stood up a bit straighter!"

My kids are adrenaline junkies, so I am used to adding at least one element of soft adventure to every vacation we take. For example, on a cruise to Alaska last year, my kids had us sign up for a "glacier hike." We went on a small biplane that took us to the edge of an enormous iceberg. Then we all climbed into kayaks and rowed around the glacier—just imagine the breathtaking beauty of being surrounded by icebergs so big, they loom across the horizon like mountains. In retrospect, I think Charlie and Gabby might have been too young to appreciate the majestic beauty of Alaska, but they enjoyed the challenge of the outing.

I am a big proponent of soft adventures; When I go just a bit outside of my comfort zone and test my mettle in the outdoors, I always feel renewed, refreshed, and reinvigorated—and so do my kids and husband. Since soft adventures often include or are based on physical activity, this is a great way to incorporate exercise into your kids' vacations! Now before you get nervous, realize that there are many ways to add a component of adventure to your vacation without letting it take over your entire trip.

First Things First: Safety Rules

Before setting off on any soft adventure, you need to review all the safety issues involved. First, most of these trips are geared to older children and those with a certain acclimation to the outdoors. Second, if you or your child suddenly hesitates before parasailing or stops mid-climb on the rock climbing wall, then you need to respect that fear. These experiences are meant to be fun, and in that way get your blood pumping and adrenaline flowing.

Here are some hard-and-fast rules to consider:

- Wear helmets, knee pads, elbow pads, and any other safety equipment necessary to protect yourselves.

- Make sure that any company, organization, or ranch is fully licensed to provide adequate safety measures.

- All instructors or guides should be well trained, and their employers should have background checks on all.

- Alert your guides to any health issues for you and your family.

- If you or any family member has allergies, make sure you bring along your own medicines or first-aid kit.

All of the organizations and adventure planners I have included here are first-rate and take your safety seriously. However, you should always be proactive and responsible, as well. A great source of information about family adventure vacations is the Web site www.goplay-outdoors.com. You will find information about adventure travel and outdoor recreation, rentals of cabins, condos, and houses, as well as details about activities, locations, and packaged trips. Another great source is Gordon's Guide (www.gordonsguide.com), which specializes in packaged family vacations. Some of the activities offered are ATV tours, bicycle and mountain biking tours, cattle drives, canoeing, dogsledding, helicopter skiing, horsepacking trips, wagon train adventures, and whale watching trips. Another fabulous organization specializing in outdoor adventures is Backroads Adventure (www.backroads.com), which organizes trips to several national parks, northern California, Maine, and other remarkable destinations in the United States.

The Total Experience

If you prefer your vacation to be one long, sustained soft adventure, many organizations offer packages and provide the whole experience, with little planning left to you.

Here are some of my favorite organized soft adventures for families. These particular outfits stand out as superior in both quality and affordability.

Wilderness Inquiry: Getting to Know the Wild Inside—and Outside

Wilderness Inquiry is a nonprofit organization with a mission to introduce people to the magic of the wilderness. I am always impressed by the staff of outdoor experts who are trained not only in outdoor skills but also on caring for and catering to all sorts of people—regardless of their age, skill level, disability, or type of family. Their family adventure camping trips "blend a relaxed pace with structured activities"— perfect for the family who wants to better know the outdoors but also relax and rest during their vacation. Recent summer trips include a three-day St. Croix Family Canoe trip; a four-day Itasca Family Adventure at the headwaters of the Mississippi River; a Junior Lakes Family Canoe Outing; four days of canoeing in the Maine woods; and a six-day tour of the Yellowstone's geysers, canyons, and lakes.

Most trips combine many activities: canoeing, swimming, hiking, fishing, and sightseeing. In winter, trips also include cross-country skiing, sledding, snowshoeing, and dogsledding. The staff provides everything from home-cooked meals to expert instruction for all of the activities. Everyone sleeps in tents and becomes part of the camping experience. WI magically keeps its prices very moderate and even offers financial assistance—how is that for trying to fulfill your mission statement! Based in Minneapolis, Wilderness Inquiry can be reached at www.wildernessinquiry.org.

Echo's Main Salmon River Raft Trip

This outdoor adventure organized by the Echo group, which specializes in river trips, is a five-day white-water rafting expedition on the Salmon River, in the Grand Canyon's deepest canyon. This trip epitomizes a soft adventure vacation for the entire family. At double the gradient of the Colorado River in the Grand Canyon, the Salmon River is a force to be reckoned with: It's eighty-four miles long and flows through pristine wilderness backcountry, past abandoned mines, homesteads, Indian sites, and the dwellings of river people who care for the historical sites of those who homesteaded in the canyon years ago. You and your family might also catch sight of fascinating local wildlife, including black bears, bighorn sheep, river otters, and birds of prey.

The river contains both class 3 (medium) and 4 (high) rapids and provides plenty of action for families of all capabilities and interests— and Echo takes kids as young as seven years old. For the most adventurous, there are inflatable kayaks that allow you to navigate through the rapids, while for the not as daring, four-man paddle rafts are provided for participation in a team effort. For simple comfort and relaxation, nothing beats the eighteen-foot self-bailing rafts, controlled by your professional guide.

The staff provides dependable safety procedures and skilled guidance and is also known for their fabulous Dutch oven meals. There is no extra charge for camping equipment or use of inflatable kayaks. Other activities to be enjoyed—depending on weather and season—include swimming, hiking, group and individual white-water rafting, exploring, and a scenic charter flight (which costs extra). For more information about specials, discounts, and trip dates, contact www.echotrips.com.

River rafting is a wonderful, challenging soft adventure, and the United States has many riveting rivers that beckon. With many river rafting guides and operations to help organize your trip, keep the following in mind as some of our country's finest rafting sites:

- Rivers within Big Bend National Park, Texas
- Colorado River: Colorado, Utah, Arizona
- Deschutes River, Oregon
- Rivers within the Glacier National Park, Alaska
- Kennebec River, Georgia
- New River Gorge, West Virginia
- Shagit River, Washington

Take Your Family to a Dude Ranch

A number of wonderful dude ranches cater to families, but one of my favorites is the Sylvan Dale, run by the Jessup family. An authentic working cattle ranch in the Rocky Mountain foothills, Sylvan Dale is located an hour's drive from Denver, Colorado. Cattle drives, overnight pack trips, horseback rides, western cookouts, Tillie's famous recipes, and legendary Jessup hospitality can give your family a wonderful western treat. Your stay can be as long or as short as you like. Accommodations are what the Jessups call "comfortable country," as is the food—"plentiful, homemade and delicious!" You can be as active or as relaxed as you like, and there are plenty of things for young people to do. If you or your kids want to really get your hands dirty, you can join the staff to move the cattle to greener pastures or help saddle and feed the horses. All packages include

- lodging with private bath and daily housekeeping services
- delicious home-cooked meals, Sunday dinner through Saturday breakfast included, served family-style
- all evening activities and entertainment
- a guided nature walk
- a horse introduction program and gymkhana (games on horseback)
- scheduled catch-and-keep trout fishing in ponds
- a fly casting lesson for catch-and-release fly fishing on river and bass ponds
- recreational facilities: swimming, tennis, volleyball, horseshoes, game room, horse riding, and hiking trails on 3,200 acres

Sylvan Dale offers specific packages for kids, depending on their age and desired degree of participation. For example, the Tenderfoot package (ages 6–12) includes the basic package plus participation in the supervised youth program: four hours of fun Monday through Friday, including daily riding instruction and western adventures such as river tubing, crafts, colt care, old-fashioned melodrama, and farm chores. In addition, buckaroos can join the overnight campout on Eagle Ridge and participate in the Friday-afternoon Gymkhana, games on horseback. Four trail rides are included in the package, one of which is the Adios Ride. For even younger kids (ages 2–4), the Lil' Cowhand package includes the basic package plus one arena ride experience if desired. Though there is no organized children's program for this age group, child care may be arranged based on availability for an extra charge. Other activities and entertainment in and around the dude ranch include trail riding, bird watching and nature hikes, swimming in the outdoor heated pool, tennis, fishing in lakes and rivers, a game room featuring billiards and Ping-Pong, hayrides, western dancing, a mountain man show, horseshoes, softball, sand volleyball, white-water rafting expeditions, and backroads tours.

The ranch also offers summer evening activities designed for the whole family to enjoy together, including hayrides, square dancing, a ranch party complete with skits and awards, campfires and s'mores, family softball, ice cream socials—all just good old-fashioned family fun. For further information, contact www.sylvandale.com.

Hundreds of dude ranches dot the western landscape of the United States. The Dude Rancher's Association, based in Cody, Wyoming, is an excellent source of specific information about many of them (www.duderanch.org). When looking you may want to inquire about activities and services available, including riding and riding instruction, cattle drives, fishing, and specialized children's activities. Here is a bird's-eye view of a sampling that cater to families:

- ❑ 7D Ranch, Cody, Wyoming: www.7dranch.com
- ❑ Averill's Flathead Lake Ranch, Bigfork, Montana: www.flatheadlakelodge.com
- ❑ Bar Lazy J Guest Ranch, Parshall, Colorado: www.barlazyj.com
- ❑ Black Mountain Ranch, McCoy, Colorado: www.blackmtnranch.com
- ❑ Colorado Trails Ranch, Durango, Colorado: www.coloradotrails.com
- ❑ Drowsy Water Ranch, Granby, Colorado: www.drowsywater.com
- ❑ Elkhorn Ranch, Gallatin Gateway, Montana: www.elkhornranchmt.com

❏ Greenhorn Creek Guest Ranch, Quincy, California: www.green-
hornranch.com

❏ Hartley Guest Ranch, Roy, New Mexico: www.hartleyranch.com

❏ Horseshoe Canyon Ranch, North Little Rock, Arkansas:
www.gohcr.com

❏ Moose Creek Ranch, Victor, Idaho: www.moosecreek.com

❏ Old Glendevey Ranch, Jelm, Wyoming: www.glendevey.com

A Multisport Backroads Adventure

Backroads Adventure is an outdoor travel group specializing in biking,
walking, hiking, and multisport adventures, with select family destinations in California and the Southwest, the Northwest (Alaska and
the San Juan Islands, Washington), the Rockies (the Canadian Rockies, Colorado, Glacier National Park, and Yellowstone), and Maine and
Prince Edward Island.

As one family described their summertime trip to Maine, "I really
understood what Thoreau meant when he said, 'Maine has everything.' " This family communed with nature and one another as they
biked, sea kayaked, and hiked along the rocky Maine coast.

This organization is, as they say, "all about being pampered." The
highly trained and skilled guides specialize in their sport or activity
while they also make sure your every need and want is fulfilled. And
because they are knowledgeable about the history, culture, and geography of each region, you and your kids will learn without even trying.

Bike rentals are now included in the one overall price, as are all other
sports equipment, including kayaks and rafts. Whether you and your
family take a three-, four-, or seven-day journey, you will always rest in
the lap of luxury. Backroads selects only premier inns or deluxe camping situations and handles all the planning, reservations, and other lo-
gistics for you. For more information, contact www.backroads.com.

> ### MONEY MATTERS
>
> Soft adventure travel tends to be expensive because of the out-of-the-way locations, expert instruction and guides, and cost of equipment. Though most trips are all-inclusive, covering accommodations, meals, and equipment, they usually don't include air travel. Also, these organizations offer a limited number of trips each year, with a limited number of spots available. You'll want to plan as far in advance as possible to ensure you get what you want.

Family Camps

Going to camp is no longer the exclusive domain of kids. Adults who loved camp as youngsters are realizing that they would like to return to camp and with their kids in tow! Over the past few years, as more and more families have shown interest in them, camps are offering family programs that will delight everyone. If your family enjoys sleeping under the stars or in tents, singing and roasting marshmallows by a campfire, you may just want to give a family camp a try. The camps are usually found in areas where natural beauty has been preserved. Meals and activities are always included, making a family camp trip economical.

Montecito Sequoia Lodge is a quintessential family camp. Located in Los Altos, California, near the Sequoia National Park, Montecito Sequoia Lodge offers organized activities for children of all ages and adults, including tennis, archery, water skiing, arts and crafts, mountain biking, canoeing, and sailing. Families stay in a main lodge, tents, or cabins. For further information, contact www.montecitosequoia.com.

Many camps offer a spiritual or religious framework or focus. Blue Star Camp in Henderson, North Carolina, in the hills of the Blue Ridge

Mountains, offers many activities, including fishing, hiking, white-water rafting, pottery, and swimming, as well as a Living Judaism program (www.bluestar.com). Camp Tecumseh, a YWCA camp in Brookston, Indiana, is a Christian-centered camp (www.camptecum-seh.org). Specialized programs such as mother-daughter quilting at Camp Lebanon (www.camplebanon.org) in Upsala, Minnesota, are also available. Other camps are set up with more freedom and luxury. At Attean Lodge in Attean, Maine, families can enjoy the wilderness but are provided with fresh ice, wood for fires, and daily maid service in one of fifteen log cabins. Activities such as hiking, fishing, canoeing, and boating are available. A good source for finding a family camp in your area is the American Camping Association (www.acacamps.org) and Family Travel Guides (www.familytravelguides.com).

Outward Bound for Families

For more than fifty years, Outward Bound has been educating youths and adults about the wilderness. Its name has become synonymous with using the rigors of living in the outdoors to help individuals face risks and challenge themselves, teaching leadership skills, confidence, and compassion. Now Outward Bound wants to do the same for families. In their words, they want to "renew and enhance [family] relationships in a physically dynamic and supportive environment." This value-driven culture permeates every aspect of their trips. Nothing is done for you; you do everything for yourselves. For this reason, children must be at least fourteen years old and adults need to be fifty or younger. You sleep under the stars in sleeping bags on the ground—no tents, and definitely no cabins. But you will see nature more intimately than ever before. Some of their recent family trips included a seven-day Colorado backpacking trip, an eight-day canoe trip through the Florida Everglades, and a dogsledding/cross-country ski trip through the Maine woods. Outward Bound trips are only for the physically fit and hardy, but they are transformative experiences you will remember for a lifetime. Contact www.outwardbound.com for more information.

Once in a Lifetime Soft Adventure:

A Volunteer Vacation

A truly remarkable, "once in a lifetime" trip to take with your family is a volunteer vacation, which seems to be a growing trend in the United States. People are heading to remote areas of the world and offering their time, services, and experience to help disadvantaged individuals, families, and communities. One organization, Cross Cultural Solutions, has developed an arm devoted to just these kinds of trips, and more and more families are signing up. Parents want to show their kids the world, introduce them to foreign culture, and teach them how to give back to the community at large. A recent trip organized by Insight Abroad was a seven-day, six-night trip to Dharmsala, India, where families worked with the local Red Cross to help build houses, care for children, and do other community development outreach. Families get to live side by side with local people and make a productive contribution to their community in just one week. Other sites around the world are in Brazil, Costa Rica, and Peru.

Another organization, i-to-i, which sends families to twenty locations outside the United States, as well as to a number of locations inside the country, offers intense cultural immersion experiences and education to its volunteers. Again, the focus is on giving back to those less fortunate by making a positive and constructive contribution. Trips to Costa Rica, Ecuador, Poland, and Romania helped local families develop a women's cooperative, provided light construction of projects, and aided a day-care center for disabled children. In the United States, i-to-i organizes volunteer trips to Indian reservations in

Montana and South Dakota and to agricultural communities in Florida and West Virginia.

Families who have taken such volunteer trips return transformed by the experience. As one mom told me, "We weren't the same after our trip to Equador. My twin sons, then age ten, returned home with their eyes wide open. Now they are so much more cognizant of the world outside their neighborhood."

Given the somewhat challenging conditions, volunteer trips are not recommended for children under the age of eight. For more information, contact www.crossculturalsolutions.com or www.i-to-i.com.

Checklist for Including an Element of Adventure

Whether you're on a family cruise, at an all-inclusive resort, or on a trip through the New England countryside, there are some surefire ways to add a little adventure to your trip, such as any of the activities I list here. You can decide on what you think would interest your children and do an Internet search to see where you can find these activities close to your location.

- ❑ Take a mountain bike excursion
- ❑ Go horseback riding
- ❑ Test your endurance on a hike
- ❑ Glide on a windsurfer attached to a parasail
- ❑ Experience the water up close in a kayak
- ❑ Take to the waves with surf lessons
- ❑ Test your mettle while white-water rafting

• *Golden Moment Rule #9* •

Manage Your Expectations

Since we plan, daydream, and fret about vacations months before they occur, it is often difficult to stay in the moment once they begin. One way to maximize your enjoyment while on vacation is to keep a reality check on your expectations. How do you keep smiling and enjoying yourselves when your six-year-old has a meltdown, your two-year-old falls asleep just as you get to the top of the Grand Canyon, and your thirteen-year-old decides there is nothing on the menu that suits her? You remember to let go and laugh. If you focus too much on trying to control everyone's behavior—or how they should feel during a certain experience—then you step out of the experience yourself and lessen your own chances of really enjoying it.

· TEN ·

Camping in
the Great Outdoors

Your soft adventure is not over yet! America began as a wild frontier, and this pioneering spirit seems to course through our veins, making us hunger for the great outdoors. And what better way to experience nature and bring a family even closer together than by a family camping trip? As one mom of three said, "My husband and I have camped forever, but we never realized that we would have more fun taking our kids along." Another mom of two kids, ages five and seven, said, "Camping with kids is so much easier than we imagined! Once we picked our campsite and set up camp, then it's all about hanging out and having fun. And what a way to get our kids to love the outdoors!" My family has shared some special times sleeping under the stars and traveling the highways of this great country of ours, and you and your family will find camping an exciting way to vacation— one that is laid back, inexpensive, and tons of fun.

Camping means many things to many people. To some, it means pitching a tent in a campsite near to home; to others, it means traveling to one of this country's magnificent national parks and hiking into the backcountry to enjoy the wilderness at its most remote and un-spoiled. In the national parks, you can find tent-camping sites; primitive camping sites, which require that you bring in all necessary supplies and equipment as no facilities are provided; and backcountry camping—literally in the great wide open. Still others think of camping as loading the family into a recreational vehicle (RV) and heading out to one of thousands of campgrounds that cater to RV travelers. Whether you want to rough it or you'd prefer the comfort of a souped-up RV or cozy cabin is your choice. One woman told me her first and only camping experience was at a campsite on Orcas Island where a hot spring tub and restaurant were twenty feet from her insulated tent: "It was perfect for us! We got to enjoy the woods and sleeping outdoors, but we also had the luxury of eating at a nice restaurant and sitting in a hot tub under the stars!" Another family shared that she, her husband, and their three boys love to visit a new national park each summer, hiking into the backcountry to test their survival skills and mettle.

As you consider a camping trip with your family, think about what you can do with and do without, and make sure you do your research on the amenities provided at different campsites. If you prefer to sleep in a cabin, make sure the campsite you have in mind provides cabins. If you are traveling in an RV, reserve ahead and ask what services are provided at the hookup site. And if your family is interested in tent camping, you need to make reservations in advance and be sure you are well equipped for the weather conditions of the time of year you will be traveling.

Campgrounds are full of ways to enjoy yourselves on vacation. Many offer swimming pools, lakes with boat rentals, fishing ponds, tennis courts, bike rentals and paths, petting zoos, playgrounds, movie rentals, game rooms, square dances, hayrides, and miniature golf. You can visit a national park, see the northern lights, fish your way across the country, visit forty-nine state capitals or a hundred Civil War battle sites. Taking your family on a camping adventure—whether by RV, minivan, or your car—will help foster a love for the outdoors in your kids!

RENT AN RV

One way to explore the open road and experience camping is by traveling in a recreational vehicle. If you don't own one, you can rent an RV that is fully equipped with bathrooms, sleeping bunks, and full kitchens containing refrigerators, stoves, and microwaves. Two of the largest national rental companies, Cruise America RV Depot and Go Vacations, Inc., have several thousand RVs in their fleets. But there are many other, smaller dealers in the RV rental business; check your local yellow pages for listings. Check out the Recreation Vehicle Rental Association (www.rvamerica.com/rvra/index.htm) for further information.

Planning a Camping Trip

When planning a camping trip, one of your first steps is to decide where, how, and when you want to camp. Consider these questions:

- Do you want to visit a particular destination—a national park, for example—and make camping part of your trip?
- Are you camping along the way to your destination?
- Do you want to set up camp in one location and make day trips from there?
- Do you want to sleep in a tent, cabin or yurt, or lodge?
- How long are you camping for—one night, a weekend, a week, or longer?

If you are traveling from one point to another and plan to camp along the way, www.campinterstate.com is a terrific Web site that lists campsites near the major highways and freeways. If you are planning on a camping trip of one to three days and are looking for a site near home, several Web sites on pages 184–85 are organized geographically. After selecting the region, you can narrow down your choices, read about different campsites, and choose one that offers the amenities and activities suited to your family. Then you can check availability and make reservations. If you're visiting a national park or particular region of the country, it's best to plan at least two months in advance, reserve a campsite ahead of time (especially when traveling to a national, federal, or state park), and learn what amenities, activities, and programs are offered during your visit.

When planning a camping adventure, you are essentially deciding among privately owned campgrounds and those that are state or federally operated. There are over a hundred national park sites across the country, and the National Park Service (NPS) offers a comprehensive Web site (www.us-national-parks.net) that can help you locate parks, monuments, trails, rivers, seashores, and even battlefields that come under its domain. You can search the Web site by activities in which you are interested, including fishing, hiking, horseback riding, and wildlife views, and plan a visit accordingly. The national parks are generally open all-year round, but most people visit in the summer. At times the parks or areas of the parks are forced to close to protect the environment and its denizens due to weather or other environmental conditions. Check well in advance and make sure some well-traveled parks are open to visitors. At all of these parks, you'll find rangers and other staff who are courteous, helpful, and very knowledgeable.

Some of the country's most comprehensive and best reviewed campgrounds are part of Kampgrounds of America (KOA campsites), a national network of private campgrounds. Most of these are well cared for, clean, and safe. Campsites are operated by their owners, ensuring on-site support and oversight. KOA's Web site (www.koakampgrounds.com) offers thousands of campsites plus helpful camping tips to make your experience more enjoyable, including links to RV rentals and reviews of individual campsites. KOA campsites offer tent camping and RV hookups; some (not all) offer lodges, cabins, and cottages. Campsites are frequently situated by the water (rivers, lakes, or ponds) and offer many activities, including horseback riding, trail riding, swimming, hiking, playgrounds, and a full range of facilities. Many of the newer (or recently updated) campsites offer wireless Internet access.

Nearly all KOAs offer a wide selection of spacious, level sites with picnic tables, water spigots, and fire pits. Many campgrounds also offer access to a free camping kitchen, electricity plug-ins, and a utility sink for dishwashing. Some KOA Kampgrounds even offer Tent Villages with a patio, windbreak, canopy cover, and lockable storage cabinets. Traveling in your own RV? Check out KOA's extensive library of articles on RV camping. You'll find a wealth of advice on what to bring, what *not* to bring, and how to keep your RV in tiptop shape.

KOA is geared toward families who are looking for a fun, safe, and bonding camping experience. The Web site offers recipes for cooking by the campfire, games to play with kids of all ages, and other practical advice for encouraging kids to get (and stay) involved in the camping experience. KOAs are generally pet-friendly.

Here are some useful Web sites that will help you plan your camping trip, locate a campsite in the area you are traveling, and find out what to expect, including amenities, activities, and the best times of the year to visit and camp:

www.campinterstate.com—easy camping while traveling the interstates

www.campsites411.com—great locator of campsites across the country

www.koakampgrounds.com—comprehensive guide to KOA campgrounds around the country

www.recreation.gov—guide to federal and state parks

www.reservations.nps.gov—to reserve a campsite at any national park *www.reserveusa.com*—to reserve at national forest campsites

www.wecamp2.com—a Web site organized by fellow camping aficionados

Camping Checklist

How much you enjoy yourself when camping often relates to how prepared you are. You can't just wing a camping trip. Once you decide where you are going, how long you are staying, and how you are camping (tent, cabin, or RV), then you can begin to plan and pack for your trip. Here are some items you should consider bringing along when tent camping. (Keep in mind that many of these items are available for rent through outdoor-sport shops.)

- ❑ tent or tents (Many families have their school-age children sleep in a tent separate from the adults.)
- ❑ tent poles
- ❑ tent stakes strong enough to withstand weather and that work in sandy soil (Put your tent up before you go to be sure you know how it works and you have all of the parts.)
- ❑ ground cloth tarp(s) to use under the tent to prolong the life of your tent and on top of the tent for extra rain protection or sun protection
- ❑ lantern(s) (I suggest using a lantern that uses rechargeable batteries—and don't forget the charger!)
- ❑ lantern tree hanger
- ❑ dependable flashlight(s)
- ❑ fire extinguisher
- ❑ baby gate to go around fire pit (if you have small children)
- ❑ gloves to pick up hot things
- ❑ matches

- ❏ small hatchet
- ❏ stake-hammering mallet
- ❏ small broom to sweep out your tent
- ❏ small rug for outside your tent door
- ❏ clothesline and clothespins
- ❏ cooler(s)
- ❏ ice
- ❏ 5-gallon water container
- ❏ food and cooking supplies
- ❏ lawn chairs
- ❏ citronella candles
- ❏ Dutch oven
- ❏ portable toilet (if you have young children and will be far from facilities)
- ❏ sleeping bags
- ❏ pillows and pillowcases
- ❏ sleeping mat, pad, or cot
- ❏ sheets and wool blankets for cold nights
- ❏ bath and hand towels
- ❏ washcloths
- ❏ laundry bag
- ❏ laundry soap and dishwashing liquid
- ❏ duct tape
- ❏ spare batteries
- ❏ Swiss Army knife
- ❏ compass
- ❏ adjustable wrench
- ❏ pliers
- ❏ knot-tying card
- ❏ nylon repair tape
- ❏ spare lantern generator
- ❏ camping scissors

- ❏ extra rope
- ❏ liquid puncture preventive and repair kit
- ❏ Sportman's Goop or seam sealer
- ❏ 3/8-inch grommet kit
- ❏ battery-operated radio
- ❏ binoculars
- ❏ camera/film
- ❏ a small cup (like the espresso/cappuccino cups in the camping department)
- ❏ all necessary personal hygiene items
- ❏ all necessary prescription medications

This list is far from complete, but you can use it for your basic needs, adding to it once you determine when and where and how long you will be camping and then subtracting those items that are not necessary. Print out your checklist and pack a good week in advance to give yourself enough time to find hard-to-locate items.

RULES TO FOLLOW FOR GOOD CAMPING (Courtesy of National Park Service)

*T*he National Park Service encourages everyone visiting its parks to be respectful of the land, wildlife, and other campers and hikers. Here is its list of recommendations:

- Don't litter . . . take along a trash bag or other receptacle for collecting your trash so that you can dispose of it properly.
- Make sure that you are using the correct type of camping equipment permitted in that area. Check with your destination ahead of time for seasonal fire or camp stove restrictions that may be in place.

(continued)

RULES TO FOLLOW FOR GOOD CAMPING
(Courtesy of National Park Service)

- Don't camp in areas where you are not permitted. These areas have been declared "off limits" to campers to protect wildlife, vegetation, or for your safety.
- Check with local park, forest, or public lands agents to see what precautions need to be taken in regard to storing food away from wildlife.
- Do not feed the local wildlife.
- Take precautions against camping in an area that may be dangerous in the case of sudden flash floods. Check with local rangers to find a safe and legal camping area.
- Remember to take along nonperishable food that won't spoil.
- Be courteous and remember that you are sharing public lands with other campers and recreationists.
- Bring along extra safety items such as water, flashlights, maps, and a cell phone or radio.

Camping Destinations by Region

New England

Acadia National Park, Maine

Camping in Acadia National Park is New England camping at its best. The vistas overlooking the rocky coast of the Atlantic, the waterways, and the lush green of the land capture the rugged beauty of this part of the country. Your family can enjoy hiking, biking, sailing, and other water activities. There are two campgrounds in Acadia National Park—

Blackwoods and Seawall. Only Blackwoods accepts reservations. Seawall operates on a first-come, first-serve basis. Campgrounds normally fill early in July through September, so plan to arrive early in the day. Public showers are available within half a mile of each campground. Campsites are in the woods, within a ten-minute walk of the ocean. There are also restrictions on how many people and cars can enter the campsite: One vehicle, six people, and two small tents or one large tent are allowed. Designated campsites accommodate RVs up to thirty-five feet, but neither campground has utility hookups. From early spring to late fall, the campgrounds provide restrooms, cold running water, dump station, picnic tables, and fire rings.

Although Blackwoods remains open during the off-season, facilities are limited to picnic tables, fire rings, pit toilets, and a hand pump for drinking water. Pets are allowed but must be on a leash at all times and may not be left unattended.

As it is New England, you need to be prepared for quick weather changes. You may begin the day wearing shorts and T-shirt and by afternoon need that fleece vest or rain jacket. Contact www.acadia.national-park.com for more information.

KOA Bar Harbor, Maine

This four-star, diamond-rated oceanfront campground has been operating for forty years. Situated only minutes from Acadia National Park, the Nova Scotia Ferry, and historic downtown Bar Harbor, it's open from May 6 to October 22. Watch seals, sail, kayak, hike Acadia, or simply enjoy one of the country's most pristine natural preserves. The Bar Harbor KOA campground can accommodate tents to the largest RVs, a new RV Kamping Lodge, and pop-up tent trailers. The resort town of Bar Harbor lies far below and the Cranberry Islands out in the bay beckon. An hourly shuttle runs from KOA to Bar Harbor in season. Whale-watching and fishing boats hire out, and restaurants specialize in lobster and blueberry pies. Or boil your own lobster in the pot back at your site. For more information, contact www.barhar-borkoa.com.

Normandy Farms, Massachusetts

Normandy Farms is a privately owned and operated exquisite camp-site, located thirty miles southeast of Boston near Cape Cod. Offering RV hookups, rental RVs, deluxe cabins (that include most necessities for cooking, cleaning, and enjoying) and more, Normandy Farms is open all year round. Reserve in advance, bring your own linens, and no pets are allowed in the rental units. Normandy Farms offers an ever-changing array of activities synchronized with holidays, such as Easter Egg Hunts in spring and special events for Father's Day. During Halloween week, kids will have a blast at the spooky hayride, costume dance, trick or treat, and a scary movie. For more information, visit www.normandyfarms.com.

Mid-Atlantic

Harpers Ferry, West Virginia

Harpers Ferry KOA Campground, open year-round, is located about sixty-five miles from Washington, D.C. Surrounded by quiet woods, this campground offers many activities as well as interesting historical edu-tainment about the Civil War. Nearby you and your family can hike the Appalachian Trail, go rafting on the Shenandoah or Potomac Rivers, or visit the Civil War Reenactment Museum or Harpers Ferry National Park, with guided tours and other programs. The campground also features an Olympic-size pool, movie theater, indoor gym, and ex-tensive activities program for kids and adults, including basketball, volleyball, organized games, arts and crafts festivals (in certain sea-sons), and much more. Tent, RV, and cabin camping are all available. Contact www.harpersferrykoa.com for further information.

Washington, D.C., NE KOA Kampground

This campsite is also located close to Washington, D.C., making it a perfect place for a family who wants to combine camping with a trip to the nation's capital. Your family can visit the many historic and cultural venues of Washington, D.C., and then camp in a beautiful natural setting. Open March 25 to November 1, the campground offers guided tours that depart for D.C. daily and free transportation to D.C.'s transit system. But the fun doesn't stop there. Six Flags Amusement Park (discount tickets available) is also nearby. Set on fifty acres of rolling countryside, the campground includes cabins, lodges, and a tree-shaded pavilion. KOA is most active during the summer months with activities from flashlight lollipop hunts, to pony rides, to line dancing and occasional wine and cheese get-togethers. Contact www.koakampgrounds.com for further information and reservations.

Shenandoah National Park, Virginia

Shenandoah National Park is set against the spectacular Blue Ridge Mountains, the Appalachian Mountains, and the Shenandoah River. Skyline Drive, a winding road that crests a part of the Blue Ridge Mountains, provides amazing vistas. You and your family can hike on over five hundred miles of trails, picnic, participate in organized activities, watch audiovisual programs and view the exhibits in the visitor centers, fish in one of thirty legal park streams, or just plain relax in the peaceful surroundings. The park also offers activities specifically geared to children ages seven and older, including Shenandoah's award-winning Junior Ranger Explorer Notebook, available for a small fee. The fifteen activities in the book guide children as they explore forest trails, streams, plants, and animals. Children draw, record observations, and answer questions. After completing a certain number of activities and attending two ranger programs, children earn a sticker, badge, or patch. Families may rent Junior Ranger backpacks containing field guides, binoculars, and other supplies.

The five campgrounds in Shenandoah National Park are geared toward tent camping. The roomy sites have picnic tables and grills, and all are near the Appalachian Trail. All except Mathews Arm have showers, laundry, and a camp store. No campground has hookups for water, electricity, or sewage, but Mathews Arm, Big Meadows, and Loft Mountain have dump stations. All are accessed from Skyline Drive.

If you'd prefer to stay inside, Shenandoah National Park has two lodges, Big Meadow Lodge and Skyland Lodge, and the Lewis Mountain Cabins. For information and reservations, contact: ARAMARK Shenandoah National Park Lodges, PO Box 727, Luray, VA 22835, or go to www.shenandoah.national-park.com.

Pets are permitted but must be leashed at all times. They are allowed in campgrounds, but not inside the lodging units, public buildings, conducted walks and hikes, and where there is a "No Pets" sign. Anglers between the ages of sixteen and sixty-five must have a Virginia fishing license through the Virginia Department of Game and Inland Fisheries at www.dgif.state.va.us.

South/Southeast

Great Smoky Mountains National Park, Tennessee

Great Smoky Mountains National Park, located in western North Carolina and eastern Tennessee, encompasses over half a million acres, making it the largest national park in the East. You can enjoy this vast and varied landscape of misty mountains, tumbling mountain streams, weathered historic buildings, and uninterrupted forest stretching to the horizon by car or on foot. Make sure you view the wildlife at Cades Cove, catch the sunset at Clingman's Dome, visit the overlook at Mile High Overlook, and check the Rockefeller Memorial at Newfound Gap.

The Great Smoky Mountain camping is primitive by design. Ten campgrounds operate in the park nestled in the woods and along rivers. All campgrounds provide cold running water and flush toilets, but no hookups. Two campgrounds, Cades Cove and Smokemont, remain open all winter. The others are open from early spring through the first weekend in November. Reservations can be made at Cades Cove, Elkmont, and Smokemont up to five months in advance, depending on the date of your stay. The remaining seven campgrounds are first-come, first-serve only.

Le Conte Lodge, which is accessible by trail only, is the only indoor lodging available in the park. It fills quickly; make reservations a year in advance. Perched atop 6,593-foot Mount Le Conte, the third highest peak in the park, the lodge is open from mid-March to mid-November. For reservations, write to Le Conte Lodge, 250 Apple Valley Road, Sevierville, TN 37862, or call 423-429-5704.

The Great Smoky Mountains Institute at Tremont is a year-round residential environmental education center that offers workshops and programs for everyone, from grade-school children to Elderhostel groups and teachers. Programs include hiking, slide shows on flora and fauna, mountain music, living history, and wildlife demonstrations. School groups, teachers, naturalists, and outdoor enthusiasts can find opportunities to hike, attend presentations by park experts, learn plant identification, tour the national park, and sing around the campfire. The Smoky Mountain Field School offers weekend workshops, hikes, and adventures for adults and families year-round. In cooperation with the National Park Service and the University of Tennessee, experts on Smoky Mountain plants, wildlife, and history lead programs.

Dry Tortugas National Park, Florida

This national park is a string of small island reefs, or keys, southwest of Miami, Florida. Named Las Tortugas (The Turtles) by Spanish explorer Ponce de León in 1513, this national park got the "Dry" part of its name because there is no fresh water available. In 1825 a lighthouse was built on Garden Key to warn sailors of rocky shoals; in 1856 the light on Logger Key was built; and by 1829 the Tortugas were fortified, to protect Atlantic-bound Mississippi River trade. The construction of Fort Jefferson began in 1846 and continued for thirty years but was never finished.

Families will find lots to learn, see, and do at this marine-oriented national park. Not least among the natural treasures are its namesakes, the endangered green sea turtle and the threatened loggerhead turtle. You and your family can choose from self-guided tours, ranger-led activities, bird- and wildlife watching, picnicking, saltwater sport fishing, snorkeling, swimming, and scuba diving.

But the park is not easy to get to. It can be reached only by boat or seaplane; it is inaccessible to trailers and motorhomes. Vessels may anchor between sunset and sunrise in a designated anchorage area, defined as the area of sand and rubble bottom within one nautical mile of the Fort Jefferson harbor light. Overnight anchoring is not permitted at any other location in Dry Tortugas National Park. The only lodging in Dry Tortugas National Park is the Garden Key Campground, which is open year-round on a first-come, first-serve basis. The thirteen-site, primitive campground is located on the same island as Fort Jefferson and is a short walk from the public dock. Eleven individual sites can accommodate up to six people and three tents each. Should a regular campsite not be available, an overflow area is provided, as well as a group site for ten to forty people, which must be reserved in advance. Call 305-242-7700 to obtain a reservation application or visit www.dry.tortugas.national-park.com. There are also lodging and services available onshore nearby in the local communities.

Blackwater River State Park, Florida

A favorite destination for canoeists and kayakers, Blackwater River in the western panhandle of Florida, outside of Pensacola, offers families many opportunities for fun and sports in the outdoors. Boasting one of the purest sand-bottom rivers in the nation, this park is a popular place for swimming, fishing, camping, and paddling. Shaded campsites are just a short walk from the river. Whether you enjoy sports and activities or quiet days of leisure, you can find what you're looking for. Enjoy a picnic at a pavilion overlooking the river or a stroll along trails through undisturbed nature. Atlantic white cedars line the river. One was recognized in 1982 as a Florida "champion tree," one of the largest and oldest of its species.

This 590-acre park offers thirty campsites with electric and water hookups as well as a dump station. All Florida state parks are open from 8 a.m. until sundown 365 days a year. Contact www.florida-stateparks.org for further information.

Midwest/Great Lakes

Muskegon KOA, Michigan

Nestled near Lake Michigan, this campsite captures the quiet, rustic natural beauty of the Midwest's Great Lakes region. Open May 1 to October 16, the campsite is situated on its own private lake, where swimmers and anglers can enjoy themselves. You can also rent a pedal boat, kayak, or rowboat. Make yourself at home in a lakeside cabin or pitch your tent on the sandy beach. RVers are also welcome, enjoying grassy, shaded sites and telephone service.

Kids will have endless fun with Saturday night hay wagon rides (kids free), volleyball, basketball, and horseshoes, and a playground for little ones. Much lies beyond the borders of the campground, including Lake Michigan's beaches, golf courses, and other popular attractions. You're close to four state parks, including P.J. Hoffmaster and its towering sand dunes. Nearby Michigan's Adventure amusement and water park are a hit with kids. In the city, tour the USS *Silversides,* a World War II submarine. Other attractions nearby include Hackley and Hume historic sites, Hackley Park Statues, Muskegon County Museum, West Michigan Children's Musuem, Craig's Cruisers Family Fun Center, and Great Lakes Downs. Contact www.koakampgrounds.com for more information.

Isle Royale National Park, Michigan

Isle Royale National Park is located on Lake Superior, about seventeen miles southeast of Grand Portage, Minnesota, and about forty-five miles north of Copper Harbor, Michigan. Known for over a hundred years as a boater's paradise, this maritime park is an oasis of family fun and activities, including canoeing, sailing, kayaking, swimming, and fishing. The exciting, challenging one- or two-day Junior Ranger program is designed for children six to twelve years of age. Kids work with their parents and rangers to solve the riddles of life on Isle Royale. Graduates are awarded a badge and certificate.

Any visit to Isle Royale will require substantial planning because the island can be reached only by passenger ferry, seaplane, or private boat. Depending on what activities you and your family enjoy, you should pack everything you will need, as there are no rentals available in the park. Although the park is open year-round, keep in mind that the park is most crowded in late July through August and less crowded April through early July and September through October.

Three types of camping are available at Isle Royale: three-sided shelters (maximum six people), tent sites (maximum six people) for one to three tents, and group sites (for parties of seven to ten people) for stays of two, three, or five nights. Long-term campground stays are not permitted. To ease overcrowding during high season, campgrounds have varying limits on consecutive night stays.

In Isle Royale National Park, lodging is available at Rock Harbor Lodge. The lodge, managed by National Park Concessions, is open May through September. Located along the shore of picturesque Rock Harbor, the lodge offers housekeeping rooms with private baths. Other facilities include a dining room, store, snack bar, gift shop, marina, motorboats, guided fishing, and sightseeing tours. For more information, write National Park Concessions, Rock Harbor Lodge, Isle Royale National Park, PO Box 605, Houghton, MI 49931-0605, or visit www.isle.royale.national-park.com for more information.

Isle Royale National Park emphasizes low-impact camping to preserve the fragile environment and not disturb the wildlife. Fires are prohibited in most areas, so self-contained stoves are a requirement. Campers must carry out all trash, not bury or burn it, or put it into pit toilets. Quiet hours are enforced, and feeding or disturbing wildlife is prohibited. Dogs, cats, and other pets are not allowed within park boundaries; neither are firearms and fireworks.

During the summer, visitors can reach the island via private ferries originating in Grand Portage, Minnesota, or Houghton or Copper Harbor, Michigan. A seaplane service also operates out of Houghton. Winter headquarters for Isle Royale National Park is located in Houghton.

Theodore Roosevelt National Park, North Dakota

"Nothing could be more lonely and nothing more beautiful than the view at nightfall across the prairies to these huge hill masses, when the lengthening shadows had at last merged into one and the faint after-glow of the red sunset filled the west," said Theodore Roosevelt, the namesake of this national park in west-central North Dakota. Located in the Badlands, Theodore Roosevelt National Park offers a smorgasbord of geologic, ecologic, and historic sites and experiences.

This area offers a fascinating glimpse into how the Great Plains and Rocky Mountains were formed. Though many of us think of the Badlands as arid and barren, in fact this park is home to many creatures and plants. Bright wildflowers contrast with the red, brown, and greens of the earth, making for a dramatic mix of color and texture. And there is no shortage of wildlife. Over 180 species of birds, many of them songbirds, inhabit the park, along with mule deer and white-tailed deer. The white-tails prefer the river woodlands, and the mule deer like the more broken country and the uplands. Prairie dogs, historically a staple food for many predators, live in "towns" in the grasslands. Through careful management, some animals that nearly became extinct are once again living here. Bison and elk, for example, were reintroduced in 1956 and 1985 respectively. Whether you are a casual observer driving or hiking through the Badlands or an amateur or professional geologist, you will appreciate the fascinating story of this rugged land.

During your visit you and your family might catch glimpses of pronghorn antelope, coyote, and golden eagles. Wild (feral) horses can be seen in the South Unit and longhorn steers in the North Unit.

This national park is open year-round. Although there is no lodging in the park, three campgrounds are suitable for tent camping. Camping is on a first-come, first-serve basis; group camping requires reservations. This national park features backcountry camping in primitive conditions. Permits are required, and it is suggested that you contact the park ahead of time to make sure about weather conditions, which can be quite extreme. Contact www.theodore.roosevelt.national-park.com.

Southwest

Grand Canyon National Park, Arizona

As one of the most spectacular examples of erosion anywhere in the world, the Grand Canyon is a breathtaking display of nature at its most dramatic. This park covers 1,218,375 acres in northwestern Arizona and is visited by almost five million people each year. With a host of activities to choose from and sights to enjoy, your family will find the Grand Canyon unforgettable.

The park offers free ranger-led programs throughout the year, including a wide variety of walks, talks, and a nightly evening program (outdoors in summer, indoors during cooler weather). There are also campfire programs and nature talks for children. Make sure you pick up the park newspaper, *The Guide,* when you arrive for details and schedules of current activities. Regularly scheduled special events at Grand Canyon include art exhibits at Kolb Studio on the rim (April–October), theatrical productions in the summer, the Grand Canyon Chamber Music Festival each September, and much more.

The Grand Canyon Junior Ranger program offers activities and programs geared for children from ages four to fourteen. Kids receive a certificate, get sworn in as a Junior Ranger, and get to wear a badge just like rangers wear. Some of the recent activities offered for kids nine to fourteen include the Junior Ranger Discovery Pack Program, during which the whole family can explore the wonders of Grand Canyon ecology; the Junior Ranger Fossil Program, a hands-on geologic and archeological dig; and Dynamic Earth, which introduces kids to how the Grand Canyon was formed.

When camping in the Grand Canyon, you and your family have four options: Desert View Campground, Mather Campground, North Rim Campground, and Trailer Village RV Park. If you prefer to sleep indoors, there are seven lodges in the park, one historic hotel, and one guest ranch. Lodging on the South Rim includes Bright Angel Lodge, El Tovar Hotel, Kachina Lodge, Thunderbird Lodge, Maswik Lodge, Moqui Lodge, and Yavapai Lodge. Lodging in the park fills up quickly, so be sure to make reservations as far ahead as possible. All lodging within the park is handled through Grand Canyon National Park Lodges. Write: Amfac Parks and Resorts, 14001 E. Iliff Avenue, Aurora, CO 80014. Contact www.grand.canyon.national-park.com for more information.

A wide variety of restaurants is available from the formal El Tovar Hotel to cafeterias at Yavapai and Maswik lodges. Tusayan offers both fast food and more formal dining. The park's peak season runs from April through October; winter holiday weekends are also crowded. Summers are extremely crowded. Grand Canyon National Park's South

Rim is open twenty-four hours a day, 365 days a years. The North Rim is closed from October to mid-May.

Big Bend National Park, Texas

The Rio Grande forms the southern boundary of Big Bend National Park as well as the international boundary between the United States and Mexico. The river borders the park for 118 miles, and has carved three major canyons, which vary in depth from 1,200 feet to 1,500 feet. The name Big Bend refers to the great U-turn the Rio Grande makes here. As its Web site describes, the river arches dramatically, creating a "ribbon of green strung across the dry desert and cutting through its mountains." Like all rivers that pass through deserts, the Rio Grande has its headwaters outside this desert. The garfish and some turtles in the river are living fossils that remind us of the area's life as a lush savannah and swamp 50 million years ago.

Here you will find great birdwatching, camping, fishing, hiking, and wildlife viewing. You and your family can enjoy Big Bend from several vantage points: sightseeing by car, by backpacking, or by river raft. Commercial float trips are available through outfitters just outside the park. Or you can bring your own or rent equipment and take on the river yourselves. Between the canyons, the Rio Grande is generally slow and quiet, but the steep, sheer-walled "Lower Canyons" make for challenging white-water rafting *not* meant for novices. Any river trips in Big Bend require a free permit, obtainable at any visitor center. The park asks that you request specific river regulations and information prior to making final plans for your trip so that things can go as smoothly as possible.

As in other national parks, Big Bend has a Junior Ranger program for youths ages six through eleven. Through activities, games, and puzzles, kids have fun as they learn. They can also earn stickers, badges, patches, and certificates.

There are three campgrounds—Chisos Basin, Cottonwood, and Rio Grande Village—and the Rio Grande Village RV Park in Big Bend.

Campsite occupancy is limited to eight people and two vehicles, or one RV plus one vehicle. Big Bend National Park is open year-round, but the most park visitors come in March and on holiday weekends, with lowest visitation in August and September because of the heat. Contact www.big.bend.national-park.com for more information.

Albuquerque Central KOA, New Mexico

This KOA campground is a gemlike oasis in the desert terrain of New Mexico. Situated just outside of Albuquerque and about an hour's drive from Santa Fe, this year-round site is perfect for a family interested in combining cultural travel with the outdoors. Your family will have tons to see and do. Close to the famous International Hot Air Balloon Fiesta (in October), this campground also offers easy access to the attractions of New Mexico's two largest cities, as well as to ancient Indian ruins, ghost towns, pueblos, and all the beauty of the Southwest. Nearby you can enjoy world-class museums, shopping, dining, a great zoo and aquarium, and a new minor league baseball team, as well as seventeenth-century Spanish churches and the Bosque del Apache National Wildlife Refuge. With the majestic Sandia Mountains in the backdrop, you can experience a first-rate campsite with a heated pool, indoor hot tub, Kamping Kabins, and wi-fi capability. It's a terrific gathering spot for groups and families with an outdoor covered café, a book exchange, game room, horseshoes, video rental, and volleyball. The campground store will keep you stocked with Native American handicrafts, such as Pueblo pottery, Kachina dolls, and dream catchers. Contact www.koakampgrounds.com for more information.

The Rockies

Bryce Canyon, Utah

Located in the southwest part of Utah, Bryce Canyon National Park contains some of the country's most interesting and wild-colored rock structures. It also offers lots of outdoor activities for you and your kids, including backpacking, biking, camping, hiking, photography, stargazing, and wildlife watching. The park has a great Junior Ranger program for kids twelve and under, including its Just for Kids games and activities related to the canyon's ecology, Moonlit Walks, Night Skies at Bryce, and a Star Party.

There are two campgrounds in Bryce Canyon. The north campground with fifty-five tent sites and fifty-five RV sites is open year-round; Sunset campground with 107 sites is closed in the winter. Lodging in Bryce Canyon National Park consists of Bryce Canyon Lodge. The lodge has 114 rooms, including suites, motel rooms, and cabins, plus a restaurant, gift shop, and post office. There is a snack bar at the General Store at Sunrise Point. Though the park is open year-round, most visitors come from June to September; attendance is lowest from December through February. The park is open twenty-four hours a day, seven days a week. There may be temporary road closures during and after winter snowstorms until plowing is completed and conditions are safe for traffic.

Coeur d'Alene, Idaho (KOA)

This KOA campground is set on a crystalline lake, in a beautiful and famous resort area, midway between Seattle and Yellowstone National Park. Lake Coeur d'Alene, which *National Geographic* magazine named one of the most beautiful lakes in the world, provides 110 miles of spectacular shoreline and 26 square miles of clear water for your family to enjoy boating, sailing, fishing, and other water activities. If you are an angler, you just might catch salmon, cutthroat trout, kokanee (salmon), northern pike, largemouth bass, smallmouth bass, crappie, perch, and bluegill.

The campground, located on sixty-two wooded acres, features tent sites, cabins, and RV rentals. There is a heated pool and hot tubs to relax in. You can also rent boats to explore the lake and creek and view bountiful wildlife, including otters, eagles, osprey, and songbirds. You and your family can also enjoy pancake breakfasts, hiking and biking trails (200+ miles), and eighteen-hole putt-putt golf. Close by is the Silverwood Theme Park, Wild Waters Waterslides, Lake Coeur d'Alene Boat Cruises, fishing, boating, canoeing, kayaking, wind surfing, water skiing, golfing, biking, as well as great outlet shopping. Due to its northern location, it is open only from April 15 to September 30. Contact www.koakampgrounds.com for more information.

Glacier National Park, Montana

Created in 1910, Glacier National Park provides over one million acres of habitat and protection for a wonderful variety of wildlife and wildflowers. The general park area was once the homeland of the Blackfoot and Kootenai Indian tribes, and many areas in the park are sacred spiritual sites. The park gets its name from the fifty-plus glaciers that it contains. It also contains over two hundred lakes or streams and over 730 miles of hiking trails. You and your family can enjoy the park in many ways, including boating, biking, camping, canoeing, climbing, fishing, hiking, photography, cross-country skiing, snowshoeing, swimming, and wildlife watching. The park is traversed from east to west by Going-to-the-Sun Road, a fifty-mile-long road that follows the shores of the park's two largest lakes and hugs the cliffs below the Continental Divide as it traverses Logan Pass. Numerous scenic turnouts and wayside exhibits allow travelers to stop and enjoy the park. Interpretive van tours highlighting Blackfoot culture originate from East Glacier and the St. Mary Lodge. Guided horseback trips are available at Many Glacier, Lake McDonald, and West Glacier. Guided backpacking and day hiking trips are available through local guides.

Glacier's weather is as varied as its landscape. In the valleys daytime temperatures can exceed 90 degrees. In areas above treeline, it is often ten to fifteen degrees cooler. Strong winds predominate on the east side of the park. Overnight lows throughout the park can drop to near 20 degrees, and snow can fall anytime. A foot of snow fell on the northeastern corner of Glacier in August 1992, so pack accordingly. You may start the day in a T-shirt and shorts and need a parka by evening.

Camping in Glacier National Park is Rocky Mountain camping at its finest! There are ten major campgrounds in Glacier, but make sure you reserve ahead of time. Most are open from May to the beginning or middle of September. Historic lodges preserve the ambience of nineteenth-century travel for twenty-first-century visitors. The lodges and inns located throughout the park provide a range of accommodations: historic grand hotels dating back to the early 1900s, modern motel-type accommodations, and rustic cabins. Reservations are strongly encouraged. Rooms book fast, especially during the peak months of July and August. Contact www.glacier.national-park.com for more information.

West Coast

Yosemite, California

Yosemite National Park encompasses almost 1,200 square miles of scenic wilderness set aside in 1890 to preserve a portion of the central Sierra Nevada that stretches along California's eastern side. The park ranges from 2,000 feet above sea level to more than 13,000 feet and contains acres of alpine wilderness, three groves of giant sequoias, and Yosemite Valley, with impressive waterfalls, cliffs, and unusual rock formations carved by glaciers.

The varied landscape offers many activities for you and the kids. Make sure you visit the Mariposa Grove of giant sequoias and the historic Wawona area; drive or hike to Glacier Point, an overlook with a commanding view of Yosemite Valley, Half Dome, and the High Sierra; drive to Tuolumne Meadows along Tioga Road and take a hike. There are also regularly scheduled ranger-led walks, talks, and evening programs, concession-operated bus tours, guided horseback rides, bicycle rentals, and Junior Ranger programs for kids as young as three years old.

The thirteen campgrounds in Yosemite National Park include: Lower Pines, North Pines, Upper Pines, and Sunnyside Walk-in in Yosemite Valley; and Bridalveil Creek, Crane Flat, Hodgdon Meadow, Porcupine Flat, Tamarack Flat, Tuolumne Meadows, Wawona, White Wolf, and Yosemite Creek outside the valley. There is a thirty-day camping limit within the park in any calendar year. Reservations are required at group camps in Wawona, Tuolumne Meadows, Hodgdon Meadow, and Bridalveil Creek. Reservations for Yosemite Valley and Tuolumne Meadows campsites can be made up to five months in advance starting on the fifteenth of the month.

If you prefer to sleep indoors, Yosemite offers a number of cabins and lodge accommodations, including the Yosemite Lodge at the base of Yosemite Falls, White Wolf Lodge, and the Wawona Hotel, as well as a number of cabins. Again, make reservations well in advance by contacting the park at www.yosemite.national-park.com.

Mount Rainier National Park, Washington

Mount Rainier National Park contains vast expanses of pristine old-growth forests, subalpine flower meadows, spectacular alpine scenery, and great opportunities to experience the wonder of the outdoors. The fifth oldest national park in the United States, Mount Rainier has the greatest single-peak glacial system in the United States, with glaciers radiating from the summit and slopes of its 14,411-foot volcano. You and your family can hike, backpack, picnic, observe the abundant wildflower meadows and wildlife from park trails, as well as fish and horseback ride. If you have the muscle, you can try some summit climbing. Evening campfire programs, ranger-led interpretive walks, and children's programs, movies, and slide programs are presented throughout the park during the summer months. In winter, guided snowshoe walks are conducted in the Paradise area on weekends. Visitors should check at information desks for current activity schedules.

Campsites are available on a first-come, first-serve basis. Mount

Rainier National Park has six developed campgrounds providing almost six hundred sites open by the end of June through mid-October. Only one campground, Sunshine Point, is open for auto camping all year round. The other five campgrounds close in September and October, depending on location and weather. Backcountry camping is permitted all year round by permit only. Cougar Rock and Ohanapecosh campgrounds operate on a reservation-only basis from July 1 through Labor Day. A fourteen-day camping limit applies to all camping within the park.

Two hotels are located in the park. The National Park Inn at Longmire, which is open year round, was built in 1917 and renovated in 1990. It offers twenty-five rooms, a full-service restaurant, and a gift shop and features a cozy lounge with a stone fireplace. The Paradise Inn at Paradise is open from mid-May to early October. Built in 1917, it offers 126 rooms, a full-service restaurant and lounge, a gift shop, and a snack bar. The large lobby features two large stone fireplaces at each end and furnishings characteristic of the rustic architectural style.

Mount Rainier National Park is open year-round. More than two million people visit each year, most from May through October. Campgrounds and inns may fill to capacity on sunny summer weekends and holidays, and parking will be difficult to find at Paradise on any sunny summer day. Schedule your summer visit on weekdays, and call for reservations at the inns. Contact www.mount.rainier.national-park.com for more information.

San Francisco North KOA Kampground, California

If you and your family want to visit San Francisco, the Napa Valley, or Sonoma Valley while camping, this KOA campground set on sixty acres of unspoiled, hilly farmland is the perfect choice. Your family will have boundless fun hiking, biking, golfing, visiting the Petaluma Speedway, or wine tasting (adults only!) in the nearby vineyards. There are also first-class spas to relax and unwind. Or you can head to San Francisco with its vast array of art, science, and cultural sites.

Choose from over three hundred spacious RV, tent, and Kamping Kabin sites, each of which comes with a picnic table and fire ring. The wooded tenting sites are convenient to the restrooms, and the nearby Kamper Kitchen provides three stovetops, three sinks with dish soap, and dining tables. If you'd prefer to stay inside, you and your family might enjoy a cozy log cabin that features log-frame beds and comfortable mattresses. The cabins are also covenient to the Kamping Kitchen. The paved grass-lined RV sites have water, 20/30/50 amp electric, and sewer hookups. Pull-throughs, cable TV, and a modem hookup site are available and able to accommodate your sixty-foot rig. Contact www.koakampgrounds.com for more information.

Once in a Lifetime Camping Trip:

Yellowstone National Park, Wyoming

One of my most memorable trips to a national park was to Yellowstone during which I had one of those never-to-be-forgotten moments in which I truly felt at peace with the world around me.

In 1872 President Ulysses S. Grant signed the act that made Yellowstone the first national park, thereby protecting it "for the benefit and enjoyment of the people." Today you may be one of three million who come each year to see Yellowstone's natural beauty. As a visitor, you share the park's 2.2 million acres with its wildlife and become part of a national effort to preserve one of the most beautiful natural wonders of the world.

The views around Yellowstone are spectacular, and the vista from Artist Point made my heart open as wide as a canyon itself. While there, you must seek out Old Faithful, as well as take in some of the highest concentration of wildlife, lakes, rivers, and waterfalls in any one area.

Yellowstone's Junior Ranger program is first rate, offering two programs for kids, one for five- to seven-year-olds and one for eight- to twelve-year-olds. Your kids will learn about grizzly bears, which live in

Yellowstone and depend on the park for future survival (which is why the track of the grizzly bear is the symbol of the Junior Ranger program). The secretive grizzly bear symbolizes all that is wild in Yellowstone. As long as greater Yellowstone is preserved, grizzly bears and other animals that depend on this rich habitat will survive.

Bigger than the states of Delaware and Rhode Island combined, the park covers 2,219,823 acres. The three "must-sees" are the Upper Geyser Basin (home to Old Faithful Geyser), the Grand Canyon of the Yellowstone, and the varied wildlife in the park. Old Faithful, which erupts every 35 to 120 minutes for one and a half to five minutes, is a must-see, but don't overlook Geyser Hill and the rest of the geyser basin. This one-square-mile basin is home to hundreds of geysers and some very pretty hot springs. Take your time and explore. Sit, relax, and watch some of the geysers. Only by doing so can you experience Yellowstone's unique thermal wonders. About four miles of boardwalks lead through the basin, providing safe access and protecting delicate features from the millions of tourists who visit each year. For your safety and the protection of the thermal features, please stay on the boardwalks.

Another impressive geyser is the Grand, which is the largest predictable geyser in the world, bigger even than Old Faithful. The Grand usually erupts every eight to twelve hours for about twelve minutes. It often stops after about nine minutes and then starts again after a minute or so. This second "burst" and any subsequent bursts are among the tallest of the eruption. Be sure to wait and see if there is a second burst.

The third noteworthy geyser is the very predictable Daisy, which usually erupts every 90 to 110 minutes for about three to four minutes. Other geysers to seek out are the Riverside, Castle, and Great Fountain (located eight miles north of Old Faithful on Firehole Lake Drive).

You may see other geysers that do not erupt predictably. "Geyser gazers" (visitors to the park who study the geysers) keep track of many of them. If they tell you that a geyser is about to erupt, you may get to see something that most visitors miss.

Also check out the pools in the basin—Doublet Pool on Geyser Hill and Beauty and Chromatic pools. If no one is walking on the boardwalk (usually early morning or late evening), sit on the bench in front of the pool and you may feel thumping as steam bubbles collapse deep inside it. Beauty and Chromatic pools, located between Grand and Giant geysers, are connected underground. Over a period of weeks one pool gets hotter and begins to overflow as the other gets cooler and stops overflowing. Then the process reverses. Usually the pool that is overflowing is the most colorful.

You and your family might also want to consider taking a ranger-led walk, which is informative and fun for people of all ages. Rangers often route their "geyser walks" so that you will get to see some eruptions. Ask about scheduled walks at the Old Faithful Visitor Center. If you catch the geyser bug, you will want to spend at least a day in the Upper Geyser Basin; if not, you will still need a half day. You can visit or call the Old Faithful Visitor Center at (307) 545-2750 to get current prediction times, which are also posted in the lobbies of the inn and lodge.

Not to confuse you with the Grand Canyon in Arizona, but Yellowstone has its own Grand Canyon. With many breathtaking vistas, make sure you go to Artist Point, Inspiration Point, or Lookout Point. Take a look beyond the pastel-colored canyon and watch for ospreys flying, and visit some of the forty-one waterfalls throughout the park.

The final "must-see" of Yellowstone is the varied wildlife. No one can guarantee that wildlife will be visible, but over the years many visitors have had luck at these areas. Visit the Lamar Valley area in the mornings and toward evening to view bears and wolves. The area from the Tower to Roosevelt has been very good for watching black bears. Moose have been seen in the area north of Roosevelt, from the Petrified Tree area to above Elk Creek. There are moose, elk, mule deer, and other wildlife along the drive from Tower Junction to Mammoth. The Blacktail Lakes area is great for watching waterfowl and birds. The ponds along the highway (Tower Junction to the northeast entrance) from Roosevelt to the Slough (Slew) Creek campground road are always great for birdwatching. Elk, moose, and mule deer have been seen from the Pebble Creek area to the northeast entrance.

The cliffs and ledges just a few miles north of Mammoth or just inside the north entrance are also great for watching bighorn sheep. You can also watch elk along this road from the north entrance to Mammoth.

Campgrounds are all located inside Yellowstone National Park. Most sites are first-come, first-serve basis; others are reservations only. Lodging in the park is handled by Xanterra Parks & Resorts. Contact them at P.O. Box 165, Yellowstone National Park, WY 82190-0165, or www.yellowstone.national-park.com. Besides tent camping sites, lodging in the park consists of cabins, hotels, lodges, and the beautiful and historic Old Faithful Inn.

A note to first-time Yellowstone campers: The weather changes quickly. Winds at Yellowstone can be quite harsh, and there are frequent thunderstorms. When you leave your site to tour the park, be prepared!

• *Golden Moment Rule #10* •

Respect Nature

*I*t is up to parents to instill and educate children about the value and beauty of the natural world. The more time you spend outdoors as a family, observing and experiencing nature firsthand, the more likely your children will grow to appreciate, protect, and preserve the natural beauty of our country.

ELEVEN

Cityscapes: Venturing to Cities with Kids

As much as I am an outdoorsy person, I am also a city person. At first, when you think of cities such as Los Angeles, Dallas, Boston, or New York, you feel intimidated by the prospect of visiting with your kids in tow. The traffic, the multitude of people, and the number of "must-see" things to do can make anyone feel overwhelmed. But I have found cities to be remarkably manageable and, dare I say it, intimate places to visit. They are alive with people, art, and culture in a more concentrated way than anywhere else. They are also full of surprises.

On a mother-daughter weekend trip to New York City, filled with visits to the theater and museums and shopping, my daughter, Gabby, and I had saved one afternoon and evening without any plans. We strolled up Fifth Avenue and happened to find ourselves in Central Park. As we walked along on that enchanting spring day, we encountered street musicians, artists painting, and in-line skaters just doing their thing. We continued meandering the hills and glades and suddenly ran smack into a wedding! Gabby and I just looked at each other and laughed. What were we going to see next? we both wondered aloud.

Could we have planned such an adventure ahead of time? Of course not. That's the magic of cities; they take you where you least expect. It's both this spirit of adventure and the cityscape itself that makes a city vacation a special—and often surprising—trip to take with your family.

Cities offer great ways to give your kids an educational experience without their realizing it. If you are planning a visit to a city, you and your kids can read up on the history and culture of some of its people before arriving. For example, if you're going to Miami, why not do a little homework and read about the huge Cuban population there? Once there, your kids might enjoy—much to their astonishment—salsa dancing at club-restaurants. Many of these club-restaurants open as early as six p.m., so you can enjoy a traditional Cuban meal and then step out on the dance floor and swing those hips. Many clubs offer free classes at this early hour—for you and the kids!

Many cities such as New York, San Francisco, and L.A. contain distinct ethnic neighborhoods that you and your family can discover together. Going to L.A.'s Chinatown for dinner is a great way to immerse yourselves in a different culture as you enjoy its shops, restaurants, and art without having to pack your passport and take a multihour flight halfway across the world.

Besides Chinatown, many cities also have "Little Italy" neighborhoods, where you'll find some of the best Italian food in the world at cheap prices. If this is your thing, make sure you find out ahead of time whether any festivals are going on. For instance, the San Gennaro festival in Manhattan's Little Italy usually takes place in September. Many cities host cultural festivals at certain times each year, with interesting and singular events, food choices, art, music, and entertainment. Once you have a destination in mind, go to that city or town's

Web site to see if there are any festivals happening during the time of your visit, or plan your visit to coordinate with a festival.

The United States offers hundreds of fascinating cities to visit, and the list of city destinations here is by no means complete, but it should give you a good start. I have not made specific recommendations for hotels in the cities described because ownership constantly changes and so do the room rates, degree of service, style of decor, and overall level of comfort. All the major search engines can direct you to hotels in any budget category, and you can often find direct links to a hotel's Web site to get a more personal look at the inside of a room, the amenities offered, and current room rates. With the recent boom in discount airlines, weekend trips to cities are now much more viable. The Web site www.Hotels.com, offers a well-organized listing of hotels in all categories—budget, moderate, and deluxe—and up-to-the-minute room rates, which often feature better prices than a hotel can offer directly.

Boston

Boston is a family-friendly, down-to-earth city, jam-packed with historical venues and sites. From the place of the Boston Tea Party, to the house in which Paul Revere was born, to the battlefield of the Minutemen, Boston and its environs will entrance your kids' imaginations. No matter when you visit, Boston has a lot going on for you and your kids to enjoy. You can take a sail in the harbor or board the famous amphibious Duck Boat and take an eighty-minute land and sea tour of Boston. On land, you will pass by the State House, Boston Common, Newbury Street, Old North Church, and other famous sites. Then the bus turns into a boat and you are launched onto the Charles River, from which you can see more of the city and harbor. You can discover Boston on foot by following the Freedom Trail, and when it's time to shop, head to Newbury Street for its array of classy and charming stores or to Faneuil Hall and Quincy Market for more kitschy items. Boston's museums offer your kids a magical experience, including the first-rate Science Museum, the Harvard Natural History Museum, the Museum of Fine Arts, and the Isabella Stewart Gardner Museum. Younger kids can let loose at the Children's Museum, where the experiential exhibits both entertain and educate.

Boston is a sports town, and there are sporting events for every season—hockey and basketball in winter, baseball and soccer during the spring and summer, and football and rowing in the fall. Boston can be cold in the winter, rainy in spring, hot in summer, and absolutely beautiful in the fall. Each season has its charm, but do prepare for the ever-changing, ever-challenging weather.

Must See: Boston Common

Must Do: Take the Duck Tour

Must Try: Clam Chowder at Durgin Park

For more information about Boston: www.bostonkids.net.

New York

Whether you are considering your first trip to New York or your tenth, there is always something new awaiting you in this marvelous, ever-changing city. While New York City is comprised of Brooklyn, Staten Island, Queens, the Bronx, and Manhattan, I am going to focus on the island of Manhattan. Marked forever and indelibly by the many immigrants who have arrived on its shores, Manhattan is still a melting pot of cultures. Carved into its landscape are its many distinct neighborhoods, including Chinatown, Soho and Tribeca, Noho and Little Italy, Greenwich Village and the Lower East Side, the vast space known as Midtown, the Upper East Side and West Side, Spanish Harlem, Harlem, and Washington Heights. Each neighborhood offers its own special eateries, from Chinese restaurants to Jewish delis, to Irish bar and grills, to Mexican, Cuban, Korean, and Vietnamese restaurants, and everything in between.

There are more museums in New York's 22.7 square miles than in any city in the United States, but some of my favorites for kids and families include the Museum of Natural History, the Guggenheim, the Metropolitan Museum of Art, MOMA, the Children's Museum, and the Museum of Television and Radio. Make sure you step inside Central Park, visit its zoo, take a ride on its hundred-year-old carousel, or rent a bike at the Loeb Boathouse. When the weather sends you indoors, your kids can stretch their legs and let off some steam at Chelsea Pier, an enormous indoor sports complex that will tire out your little and big ones. Golf, swimming, in-line skating, basketball, and running are all available. A number of kitschy bowling alleys, such as Bowlmor down on lower Broadway, can also be fun. It's easy to get around New York— whether you walk, take a bus, hop on the subway, or flag down a cab. You'll want to take your kids to see these historic and cultural sites no family should miss: the Empire State Building, Rockefeller Center, Grand Central Terminal, and St. Patrick's Cathedral. It's also fabulous to see New York from the water. The world-famous Circle Line circles Manhattan, providing spectacular views of the city's architecture and bridges. You can hop a ferry to see the Statue of Liberty. New York's climate follows Boston's change of seasons but is milder in winter and hotter in summer, so come prepared.

Must See: Lower East Side Tenement Museum

Must Do: Visit the Intrepid Sea Air Space Museum

Must Try: A hot dog loaded with onions, kraut, and relish from a street vendor

For more information about New York: www.newyorkkids.net.

Philadelphia

For such an important historical city, Philadelphia is small and inviting. A ninety-minute train ride south from New York's Penn Station, Philadelphia is easy to access, and your family can enjoy its many sites in a short two-day weekend. You can start your walk back into American history with a visit to the homes of Ben Franklin, Betsy Ross, and William Penn, the city's chief architect. If you would rather not walk, take the ninety-minute narrated trolley trip that offers a complete tour of the city and allows you to hop on and off at designated stops along the way. Your kids will also appreciate the Museum of Tolerance, which offers kid-oriented exhibits on slavery and civil rights, the Holocaust, and stories of overcoming immigrant prejudices. Walking the cobblestone streets through Rittenhouse Square or the Italian Market, you can feel the historic presence of the city come to life. Philadelphia's climate is similar to New York's with its four seasons.

Must See: Liberty Bell
Must Do: Nighttime walk of the Founding Fathers
Must Try: Philly cheesesteak

For more information about Philadelphia: www.philadelphiakids.net.

Memphis

Most of us think of Memphis and think of one person: Elvis. Of course, Elvis is a huge part of this southern city's heritage, but there's lots more to see in addition to a visit to Graceland. Its famous Beale Street is lined with bars, music clubs, and dance halls and is a testament to this city's place in the history of blues music. It's safe and easy to walk around, and kids will enjoy the statue of Elvis in front of the Orpheum Theater, the Rock 'n' Soul Museum, run by the Smithsonian, and the Gibson Beale Street Showcase, which gives great thirty-minute tours of its guitar factory. Your family will also take pause at the National Civil Rights Museum, located on the very site where the Reverend Martin Luther King, Jr., was shot and killed. The *Memphis Queen* is a great way to experience the Mississippi River and see Memphis by boat. The Memphis Zoo is also home to two pandas—YaYa and LeLe! And don't forget your tour of Graceland—Elvis is buried by the pool. Although Memphis has a winter, it does not get as cold as northeastern cities, but it gets quite hot during the summer, and sometimes even in late spring and early fall.

Must See: Graceland

Must Do: Attend the Reverend Al Green's Full Gospel Tabernacle Choir church service

Must Try: Tops Bar-B-Q

For more information about Memphis: www.memphissite.com.

Indianapolis

Indianapolis, Indiana's capital, is a vibrant, bustling city brought alive by its Indianapolis Motor Speedway, home of the Indianapolis 500 motor race, which takes place every year over Memorial Day weekend. Though tickets are difficult to get, NASCAR fans will enjoy the Hall of Fame Museum, which contains seventy-five racing cars, including former Indy winners. Sports enthusiasts might also enjoy a visit to the NCAA Hall of Champions. Younger kids won't want to miss the Children's Museum, which has a hands-on world of discovery, including a limestone wall for climbing, sailboating on an indoor river, and one of the largest displays of family dinosaur fossils in the world. Kids can even dig for dinosaur bones. At the Connor Prairie kids can go back in time and experience life on an nineteenth-century farm. Visitors dress in clothing of that time, spend the night at one of the homesteads, and cook their own meals. They can watch period actors plow fields, manage the animals, sing and play music, or pitch in and do chores! Indianapolis is seasonal like New England, but with less extreme temperatures.

Must See: Hall of Fame Museum
Must Do: Glow-in-the-Dark Cosmic Bowling at Expo Bowl
Must Try: Old-fashioned ice cream soda at Fountain Square

For more information about Indianapolis: www.indy.org.

Chicago

Chicago loves kids and kids love Chicago. From its Museum of Holography, where kids can see the world's largest collection of holograms (three-dimensional imaging), to its Blue Chicago Store, where kids can listen to a live blues band perform in a smoke- and alcohol-free space, to its Shedd Aquarium, to its Museum of Science and Industry, which has model trains running on 3,500 square feet of track, kids will be entertained for days! One of Chicago's most special places is the American Girl Place, which gets more than 100,000 visitors every year. It offers theater and tea parties where girls can be seated with their dolls. Some hotels also package trips with American Girl Place. If the boys get a bit bored by this girly venue, entice them with a visit to the Lego Store, where kids can build their own creations. For more sophisticated cultural sites, check out the John Hancock Center, the Navy Pier, the Field Museum, and the Adler Planetarium, and take a stroll down the

Magnificent Mile for some fabulous shopping. Chicago is cold in winter, with bone-chilling winds sweeping across Lake Michigan, and truly hot in summer. Spring and fall are wonderful months to visit.

Must See: Wrigley Field

Must Do: See a live recording of an *Oprah Winfrey Show*

Must Try: Ribs at Carson's

For more information about Chicago: www.chicagoparent.com.

San Antonio

I think of San Antonio as the heart of Texas, with its gracious Riverwalk at its center. You and your family can cruise or walk to get a keen sense of the leisurely, laid-back culture of this Tex-Mex city. For a bit more action, you can visit the Alamo. This eighteenth-century mission was the site of one of Texas's (and America's) bloodiest battles, and by walking its grounds your family will be able to take in a big slice of history. South of the Alamo are a few more missions that bring Texas's ties to Mexico alive. The Mission San Jose and Mission Juan Capistrano are a must. Market Square is a great place to shop, and the Tower of the Americas, built for the 1969 World's Fair, is one of the tallest points in Texas. Kids will feel challenged at the Witte Museum's HEB Science Treehouse, where they can hoist themselves up a four-story atrium by a pulley. The museum also has a first-rate dinosaur reproduction, a mummy, and an eco lab of live Texas animals. Every April is the huge Fiesta San Antonio, a nine-day, citywide multicultural extravaganza. Texas is fully air-conditioned for one main reason: Its heat is unrelenting, and San Antonio is at the heart of this hot zone. From mid-April to mid-October, San Antonio is hot and humid. Its winters and springs are mild and pleasant.

Must See: The Riverwalk

Must Do: Visit the Alamo

Must Try: Dinner at Magic Time Machine

For more information about San Antonio: www.sachamber.org.

Seattle

This temperate, laid-back city is a wonderful place for children and families, and it is surrounded by some of the most magnificent land-scapes in the country. All you have to do is look up to see the white-caps of the Cascade and Olympic mountain ranges and then west to the Puget Sound to take in the beauty of the many islands that dot the waterways. Take your kids first to see Pioneer Square and the totem poles of Occidental Park. Then go to Pike Place Market to eat or shop, hop on the monorail to climb the Space Needle, and then head to the Klondike Gold Rush National Historic Park. Your kids will love the Pacific Science Center, with virtual reality exhibits, laser shows, holograms, and a planetarium. The Seattle Aquarium will show kids the sea life of the waters off the city, and next door is the Imax Dome, which shows an IMAX movie of the eruption of Mount St. Helens; you can see the actual mountain off in the distance. Your family will also enjoy Boeing's Museum of Flight, which offers hands-on exhibits for kids and a life-size replica of an FAA control tower. North of Seattle is a picturesque Bavarian village named Leaven-worth.

Seattle has a temperate climate, and it rarely gets uncomfortably cold or hot. It does rain, however, and very often, so come prepared. Because of its northern position, late spring and early summer are wonderful times to visit, as it stays light into the night.

Must See: The city from the top of the Space Needle

Must Do: Take a ferry ride to one of the islands off the coast

Must Try: Coffee at the first Starbucks

For more information about Seattle: www.seattlekids.net.

Los Angeles

Everyone in the family will have a ball in Tinseltown. Los Angeles is full of entertainment-related venues, outdoor activities, interesting cultural events and museums, and lots of great dining experiences. Your kids will love to visit or tour Sony Pictures Studio, Universal Studios Hollywood, or Warner Bros. Studios. If you're in the mood for more rapid recreation, head to Disneyland. The Hollywood Guinness World of Records is a great place to take the whole family. You might even be able to get on the set of a game show.

Given L.A.'s temperate climate, you and the kids can discover another part of Southern California at one of the many beach towns that border the city. From Malibu to Santa Monica to Venice, each beach community offers its own array of activities, including surfing, beach volleyball, biking, in-line skating, and even weight lifting (at Venice's famous Muscle Beach!). You can be a spectator or join in. Your kids will be wowed by the art, architecture, and panoramic vista from the Getty Museum, which now offers a free IPod-like, hand-held media device that guides you through the museum's collection. And you'll want to include a stop at the La Brea Tar Pits next to the L.A. County Museum.

Must See: The Walk of Fame

Must Do: Visit the Bob Baker Marionette Theater

Must Try: Burger and fries at In-N-Out Burger

For more information about Los Angeles: www.seemyla.com.

Once in a Lifetime City:

London

London is a quick five-hour flight from a number of East Coast cities and can be a magical trip for any family. Because English is spoken, this European city is especially easy for Americans to reach and get around. It has five international airports, an efficient road network, and extensive Underground (their subway), train, bus, and taxi services.

Although London is a vast city containing more than 7 million inhabitants, it is often described as a collection of villages. Its many distinct neighborhoods, each with a unique flavor and personality, contain their own signature shops, markets, parks, and other venues. Chelsea, with King's Road as its center, is known as the place where punk rock was born. You and your kids can still enjoy great people watching, and you might even catch sight of a few celebrities who live in the area—Hugh Grant or Liz Hurley, for instance. Notting Hill, made famous by the movie of the same name, used to be a shady Bohemian enclave. Now it's superhip and trendy, with eclectic shops and art galleries. Make sure not to miss Portobello Road, which is lined with antique shops and old bookstores. Bloomsbury is London's intellectual center and takes its name from the world-renowned Bloomsbury group, a coterie of writers and intellectuals of the early twentieth century. You will also find both the British Museum and British Library in this neighborhood. West End is the theater district, as well as home to smaller neighborhoods such as Soho, with film companies, charming small hotels, and great Indian food.

As a historical and cultural mecca, London will give kids a nonstop learning experience without their ever realizing it. Four sites in London are designated World Heritage Sites: the Palace of Westminster, the Tower of London, Maritime Greenwich, and Kew Gardens. With more than seventeen museums in London alone, make sure you take the family to the Tate Gallery, the Royal Academy, the National Portrait Gallery, and the Queen's Gallery in Buckingham Palace. Since London is a theater town, there are always a number of first-rate plays being produced. You will also need to visit Shakespeare's Globe Theatre. Other riveting attractions include Madame Tussaud's Wax Museum, the London Dungeon, and the changing of the guard in front of Buckingham Palace. You can also see London by air on the London Eye, the world's largest Ferris wheel, or by boat and road on the amphibious London Duck Tour. If your kids are into sailing, they may want to board the centuries-old *Cutty Sark* and get an up-close view of what sailing used to mean.

London is also a shopping haven. The whole family will enjoy Harrod's, the world-famous department store, and the many boutiques and shops throughout Covent Garden. Your kids will go wild in Mystic Fairies, a special shop where they can buy everything to do with magic, from wands, to toadstools, to broomsticks. Not to be outdone, the Forbidden Planet is the United Kingdom's largest science fiction and fantasy store, with an array of toys and gadgets having to do with *The Lord of the Rings, Star Trek,* and, of course, Harry Potter.

Tired of urban living? Take a break in one of the many park spaces around London. London contains more parks and green space than any other city of its size in the world. You can also arrange day trips outside London to Oxford and Cambridge, home to the world-famous universities, as well as to Windsor Castle, the nine-hundred-year old home to the queen's family of Windsor. The castle offers organized tours and programs for kids. A fifty-five-minute train ride from London, Windsor Castle is also accessible by bus or car. For more information, contact www.windsor.gov.uk.

Must See: The Tower of London

Must Do: Ride the London Eye

Must Try: Fish and chips

For more information about London: www.kidslovelondon.com.

• *Golden Moment Rule #11* •

Picture This

When on vacation with our family, it's easy to get caught up in a frenzy of picture taking. We all can recall the frustration of seeing our loved ones framed by a beautiful setting and rushing to the camera, wanting to capture the moment for posterity, yet being unable to get the film in the camera, the angle correct, or the lens in focus. And just as suddenly as the picture presents itself, it disappears—your three-year-old starts crying, your husband moves on, and you are left agonizing about missing the moment. Be easy on yourself. In the end, it's more important to stay present and enjoy your vacation than get stuck trying to capture these moments on film.

Cities are magical places that encourage kids to explore both the world around them and the world within them. Cities challenge us to think, grow, and push beyond the limits of our experience. The next time you're passing through, stop and take a day or two to walk around, see the sights, and discover another part of yourself.

. TWELVE .

Hidden Treasures in America's Landscape

Every person and every family define a vacation experience differently. For some, time spent at home in one's own backyard, grilling on the barbecue while the kids run around the neighborhood is the quintessential form of relaxation. Other families have more of a thirst for adventure and challenges that take them to places far from home. Still other families like to crowd themselves into a car and ramble. One family I know—a single father and his four sons—love to pile into an old VW pop-top van and meander across the states with no particular destination in mind, just a map and a general route. One year they traveled west to east across Route 66, dipping down to New Orleans and picking up Route I-10. Before heading home to Atlanta, Georgia, they decided to veer off their path and stop in Huntsville, Alabama, to visit the U.S. Space & Rocket Center, a combination science museum and theme park. This spur-of-the-moment side trip became one of their favorite parts of their entire vacation.

In this chapter you will find my special cache of hidden treasures—those slightly off-the-beaten-path venues or destinations that provide magnificent fun, spectacular sightseeing, and memorable surprises that sustain family lore for generations. You can use this listing of hidden treasures any way you want: as a primary destination for a short excursion, as a side trip along the way to your primary destination, or as a way to add either an educational or soft adventure element to your overall vacation.

Regardless of how these hidden treasures work into your trip, I guarantee that everyone will enjoy the time discovering such quintessential Americana.

Kennedy Space Center in Cape Canaveral, Florida

The next time you plan a visit to Disney World or Orlando, put the Kennedy Space Center on your must-see list. A quick forty-five minutes away from Orlando, the Space Center transports you to another galaxy! It not only captures a riveting dimension of American history but also invites the whole family to participate in a grand scientific adventure.

You can make this a one- or two-day stop, and I guarantee the entire family will have fun. Kids and adults alike can participate in astronaut training experience, which is a daylong program. What does it feel like to be in a zero-gravity space simulator? Find out! What about joining a Mission to Mars program, which is a fabulous interactive theatrical production for young kids? Also, every day you can sit down and have lunch with a real live astronaut and participate in discussions about space. Kids and adults can also climb and explore actual spacecraft.

The Kennedy Space Center also has several IMAX theaters with great films of outer space and exhibits that give you a hands-on experience of a space mission.

Contact the Space Center (www.nasa.gov) directly to find out about special events and programs and scheduled launches so you can time your visit accordingly. Kids will go wild when they participate in the excitement of a real launch.

Cape Canaveral is also the home port for several cruise lines, including Disney, Norwegian, and Carnival. All of you may enjoy the drama of watching these massive ships move in and out of Port Canaveral. You can spend an entire day watching the boats come in! Or spend the day at the Space Center before departing on your own cruise.

Catalina Island, California

This rustic, barely touched island off the coast of Los Angeles is an easy boat ride from Long Beach (about thirty miles south of Los Angeles). You can either take a high-speed boat—they leave all day, every day—or take a chartered sailboat. And indeed, getting there is half the fun! On the way over, you can enjoy the vistas of the Pacific and cliffs of Southern California, and, depending on time of year, you might see some wild marine life, including dolphins, whales, and seals!

Catalina is as quiet and rustic as you can get in California, with plenty to do for a one-, two-, or three-day hiatus. You will feel as if you have been transported back in time to before California became an overgrown metropolis. The waters of the Pacific are still a clear greenish blue and the pace is slower. An indigenous population lives on island year-round, giving Catalina a unique personality. Many people get around the island by golf cart, and it is not unusual to see people riding horseback.

Also, the island is home to a herd of wild buffalo that were let loose after they were used in a film in 1924. The island's nature conservancy offers guided tours, courses, and other events to introduce all its visitors to its rich natural preserve. Music and art festivals dot the annual calendar, so be sure to check the island's official Web site, www.catalina.com, before your visit.

The island offers outstanding snorkeling, diving, camping, and golf. Since cruise ships port here, there are a number of good restaurants and places to stay. Accommodations range from rustic to rather fancy. You can surely find something comfortable for your heads and your wallet. Contact the island's Web site for more specific information on lodging, dining, activities, and year-round festivals.

Molokai, Hawaii

Molokai, one of Hawaii's smaller islands, is as exotic and tropical as you can get while still having the arms of Uncle Sam wrapped comfortably around you. In other words, even though you are thousands of miles away from the mainland United States, you can still wake up and watch a football game on Sunday morning!

And yet for all its ties to America, Molokai feels worlds away from the hustle and bustle. It's a twenty-minute airplane ride from Oahu or a ferry ride from Maui. Once you land, you feel as if you've been dropped into a verdant jungle—safe and sound, mind you, but absolutely removed from civilization. Obviously, a trip to Molokai is no quick side trip. It deserves its own special one- or two-day visit. Molokai captures a special feature of Hawaiian history. Its indigenous people are proud of their unique culture and even protested the arrival of a fast food restaurant so that it eventually shut down.

Molokai is home to one of my favorite places—the Molokai Ranch. The people who run the ranch are some of the warmest folks I have ever met. Everyone is an auntie or uncle. While the ranch is upscale and luxurious, accommodations on Molokai run the gamut. You can rest your head in more, shall we say, *natural* surroundings: canvas-thatched "tentalos" are also available on the beach.

Just imagine celebrating all that natural beauty, watching the sun go down and then rise the next morning. I had one of my favorite Golden

Moment experiences in Molokai. I was sitting on the beach while the kids were riding waves and body surfing on a quiet cove. As I watched Gabby and Charlie, I noticed a seal's head pop up—it was as if he had come to enjoy the waves with the kids. And at the very same moment, a whale breached in background. The image—all of it—literally drew me to tears.

For more information, contact www.molokai-hawaii.com.

Cooperstown, New York

Many of you may have heard of Cooperstown because it is home to the Baseball Hall of Fame. Indeed, this rather small town is fairly smitten with anything and everything having to do with baseball. For this reason, I find a visit to Cooperstown one of those priceless pieces of Americana that no family should skip over. Of course, it may appeal at first to fathers and sons—but even my daughter and I enjoyed ourselves one summer visit a couple of years ago.

Because baseball is such an American sport, you begin to see and experience the history of this country through the eyes of all who played the game. Baseball culture, history, the players, and the way the game itself has changed and evolved over the years acts as a kind of mirror of our nation's very own history. The Little League Museum, the Baseball Hall of Fame, and other libraries and smaller exhibits will keep you entranced for hours.

If you live or are staying in New York City, you can make Cooperstown, a four-hour drive from there, a day visit. Stay the night and enjoy some of the village's quaint B&Bs, flea markets, and great antique shops. The drive north will also be a feast for the eyes, as you pass rolling hills and wide-open farmland.

The best time to go is late spring, summer, and early-fall weekends when the leaves begin to turn. And remember, there is enough to keep you busy even if not everyone in the family is a baseball fan. Contact www.cooperstown.com for easy-to-follow directions and guides to accommodations.

St. George, Utah

An hour-and-a-half drive from Las Vegas, St. George is an often overlooked treasure trove of sporting and outdoor entertainment, natural beauty, and leisure activities for the entire family.

St. George is home to Zion National Park, with its immense redrock canyon, winding Virgin River, open land, rocky streams, and waterfalls. The park is now so popular in summer that it is closed to cars. Instead it shuttles visitors via bus.

At the city center, an enormous Mormon temple stands grandly. St. George is a sports mecca, with sporting events including the St. George Marathon and the Huntsman Senior World Games. The city has devoted miles of trails for hiking, biking, and running. The Sand Hollow Aquatic Center, which is owned and operated by the City of St. George, is open to the general public and includes a competition and diving pool and a 5,800-square-foot leisure pool. The leisure pool has a zero-depth entry area, interactive children's water fun toys, a water walk, and waterslides. Various sprays and moving water provide the ultimate aquatic experience for the entire family. Outside the city, you and your family will find ten golf courses and several spas, including the world-class Green Valley Spa.

In the summer St. George really rocks, with the Tuacahn Ampitheatre offering Broadway musicals with elaborate sets and costumes framed dramatically by the red rocks. The Tanner Ampitheater is the home to wonderful musical spectacles and shows—from country to jazz to folk and rock. Dutch oven dinners can be purchased for perfect family evening festivals all summer long. For further information, contact www.utahstgeorge.com.

Wisconsin Dells, Wisconsin

You would never believe that such a place exists until you drive twenty miles outside of Madison, Wisconsin. And there before your eyes is a vast indoor complex of resorts, water parks, shopping, and dining experiences—think Las Vegas without casinos.

Interconnected themed resorts (many contain water parks) offer families a huge selection of lodging, dining, and recreation options. From the Rain Tree Resort to the Kalhari Resort to the Bay of Dreams at Mt. Olympus, your kids—and the kid in you—will feel entertained just walking around.

Wisconsin Dells is a megacenter of activities and entertainment for families—all year long! Can you imagine your kids inside on a snowy midwestern day, donning their bathing suits and careening down a waterslide? What about organizing a family competition in super mini golf courses? And you can't miss the water ski shows! Younger kids will enjoy the Tommy Bartlett Exploratory, while older kids will be enthralled by the Wizard Quest.

If you are in need of pampering, there is plenty to choose from. While your kids are plummeting down the waterslide, the Point of No Return at Noah's Arc (its motto is "Ten stories up, five seconds down"), you may want to sneak away for a massage, facial, or quick mani-pedi at the Sundara Spa, an upscale, elegant world-class spa you wouldn't expect to find in the middle of Wisconsin. The spa uses organic foods and treatments from products indigenous to the area.

The shopping will also keep you busy, with great antique shops and other kitschy shops to browse. The range of dining options is really formidable—from a vegetarian restaurant to a five-star steak house. All restaurants are known for their hearty portions, and the fried cheese is abundant!

This year-round destination is a great place to stretch the family dollar. Most of the resorts offer package deals, and accommodations come with water parks admissions.

Outdoor activities abound. The scenic limestone formations carved by the Wisconsin River invite you to take a boat tour or walk the trails around Mirror Lake or Devil's Lake. Sports include horseback riding, cross-country and downhill skiing, and snowboarding.

While you're in Wisconsin, you don't want to miss the Circus World Museum. Twenty miles northwest of Madison is the former winter home of Ringling Bros. Circus. Now the Circus World Museum, this step back in time houses a collection of wagons, posters, and equipment from the original touring days of the circus.

For more information on special events, festivals, and accommodations, contact www.wisdells.com.

Fredericksburg, Texas

Nestled in the Texas hill country, this authentic German town is a wonderful spot for a family destination. Led by John O. Meusebach, German immigrant families settled Fredericksburg in 1846. The National Historic District is made up of several older buildings that still retain the traditional styles of Germany, and many of the homes take on this old-world charm.

In the heart of Fredericksburg is the Marktplatz, which has many wonderful restaurants and tempting shops. Also within walking distance are interesting historical sites, including the Pioneer Museum Complex and the George Bush Gallery of the National Museum of the Pacific War.

Just outside Fredericksburg are Enchanted Rock State Park and the LBJ Ranch, with tons to do, including hiking, mountain biking, and river rafting down the Guadalupe River. In the spring the beautiful and colorful wildflowers are a sight to behold—vivid reds, blues, lavenders, yellows, and oranges dot the landscape for miles. Your family can enjoy antiquing along the backcountry roads or picnicking in the meadows and on the hillsides. Fredericksburg is host to many fairs and festivals during most seasons, except winter. Its most special and famous event is the Octoberfest. You and your kids will learn how to have great party German-style. Listening to the sound of oompah, smelling the aroma of sizzling bratwurst, and hearing the cries of *"Gemütlichkeit!"* will get anyone—German or not—in the mood to celebrate! For three full days each fall, the whole world is invited to sing, toast, and dance at one of Fredericksburg's favorite festivals! For more information, see www.fredericksburg-texas.com.

Leavenworth, Washington

Located two and half hours from Seattle is a wonderful village called Leavenworth. In the 1960s, the citizens here decided to construct a model Bavarian village, and since then it has become a popular northwestern tourist attraction. Fun activities abound all year, including festivals, rafting, biking, a petting zoo, horse-drawn wagon, sleigh rides, hiking, golf, and a kidfest over the Fourth of July. And during winter, when the weather cooperates, there is often cross-country skiing, so come prepared to take the whole family out in the snow! For more information, contact www.leavenworth.org.

Hershey, Pennsylvania

"The sweetest town on earth," Hershey is a one-stop vacation paradise for families. Its amusement park was recently rated number one in the Northeast by *FamilyFun* magazine, but the excitement doesn't stop there. You and the kids will enjoy trolley rides, the Hershey Museum, Hershey Gardens, the zoo, shopping, and, of course, Hershey's Chocolate World, where everyone can sample some of the world's tastiest chocolate. The amusement park has more than sixty rides, including ten thrilling roller coasters, six drenching water rides, and more than two dozen kiddie rides. With live entertainment daily, a dolphin and sea lion show, and other games, by the end of the day you will want to lay your head at the fine Hotel Hershey or the more comprehensive Hershey Lodge, or camp at the Hershey Highmeadow Campground. This special all-American town has something for everyone, including a spa and golf club. The town of Hershey is a convenient drive to so many major cities that is a terrific choice for your family reunion, too. For more information, contact www.hersheypa.com.

Road Trips Across America

There are so many ways to see the United States if you and your family enjoy piling into your station wagon, SUV, or motor home that you may want to consider these itineraries:

The East Coast

Take I-95 from Miami to Maine—this interesting and varied highway goes through major cities like Washington, D.C., New York, and Boston, and also veers you toward wonderful coastal getaways including Savannah, Georgia; Hilton Head, North Carolina; the Maryland shore; and Philadelphia.

The West Coast

Travel up or down the famed Pacific Coast Highway—from Tijuana, Mexico, to Seattle, Washington, this glorious highway cups the Pacific Ocean for about 1,500 miles.

The Middle of Everywhere

Route 66 stretches from Chicago through St. Louis into Oklahoma to Texas, through New Mexico and Arizona, and then shoots west toward Los Angeles. This legendary highway is mentioned in countless songs, movies, and TV shows and is affectionately called "Main Street, U.S.A."

The Grand Ol' Mississippi

Follow the Mississippi River from Minneapolis through St. Louis to Memphis and Natchez and down into New Orleans.

The Blue Horizon

Blue Ridge Parkway spans the majestic Blue Ridge Mountains through Appalachia. Along the way you can stop off in the Shenandoah National Park; Charlottesville, Virginia; and Asheville, North Carolina; and end your sojourn in the Great Smoky Mountains National Park.

Once in a Lifetime Hidden Treasure:

Canada

Canada is a big place, almost as big as our dear old U.S. of A., but sometimes we overlook our neighbor as a grand and exciting destination. A quick trip over the border will yield some wonderful hidden treasures. Here is a highlight of my favorite destinations—from West Coast to East.

Vancouver, British Columbia

Vancouver is a fun, laid-back city with amazing architecture, shopping, and sightseeing opportunities. On my visit one June, the sun didn't go down until ten p.m. The kids loved the novelty of staying up late outside in the light nighttime sky! Vancouver is also the beginning of the Sea to Sky Highway, which winds through five different biogeoclimatic zones from the coastal rain forest at Horseshoe Bay, through Squamish, Garibaldi Provincial Park, and the mountains of Whistler. The Sea to Sky Highway also intersects two historic routes, the Pemberton Trail and the Gold Rush Heritage Trail. We took the highway to Whistler, which in winter has phenomenal skiing. In late June, the area is prime territory for hiking, taking helicopter rides over the mountains, and picnicking. Whistler is famous for its abundant wildlife. You might see a Whiskey Jack swoop down or a black bear meandering across a meadow. You can also head farther into the wilds on a hiking or bear watching tour, or go backpacking or camping high in the mountains.

Calgary

On the other side of the Rocky Mountains is one of Canada's most interesting cities. Very sophisticated, with its own unique personality,

Calgary hosts many festivals throughout the year showing both its frontier, Wild West side and its educated, sophisticated side. You get an authentic and very real taste of the history of this frontier city. One of the biggest draws is the amazing Calgary stampede. My kids were wild about the rush of cattle through the streets! Each year millions of visitors from around the world come to Calgary to partake in this summer event, where you can enjoy real rodeos, a midway, shows, and much more. The city of Calgary is transformed for ten days into a celebration of cowboy culture. Calgary is also home to one of the most modern motorsport facilities in North America. You can rent a race car and try the triple-track complex, which features a half-mile, high-banked oval for stock car racing, a quarter-mile NHRA drag racing track, and a two-mile course for sports car and motorcycle racing.

Banff

The famous town of Banff is located in the center of Banff National Park in Alberta's Rocky Mountains. Located an hour and a half from Calgary, Banff is also a short trip from the mountain areas of Lake Louise and Canmore. Banff offers everyone in the family a ton to do: luxury escorted motor coach tours; adventure tours featuring skiing, snowboarding, rock climbing, white-water rafting—the list is endless, from bathing in hot springs to arts festivals. You will also find activities outside the norm, such as cave tours of aboriginal peoples, tobogganing, and scuba diving and snorkeling in rivers. See www.discoverbanff.com.

Montreal

Montreal offers American families the European travel experience without the hassle, or expense, of going to Europe. Located in French-

speaking Quebec, Montreal feels like a small French town, where locals gather in cafés to sip coffee and chat. The food is stupendous—
especially if you enjoy French cuisine. Even if your kids don't, they will
enjoy the pastries that can be found in the ubiquitous bakeries. Of
course, if you're a fan of Celine Dion, you will be able to see where she
was born, went to school, got married, and gave birth! Montreal loves
Celine!

Rich in culture and history, Montreal also offers fascinating festivals in the arts—music, literature, and visual arts. For information on
lodging, special events, and other travel options, contact www.mon-
treal.com.

Prince Edward Island

Off the coast of Nova Scotia is this enchanting island caught back in
time. Known for its red-clay beaches, Gulf Stream–fed waters, and
quaint cottages, it's also the home of Anne of Green Gables! There is
much for laid-back families to enjoy. I would recommend that you visit
during the summer, PEI's most inviting season, when the temperatures

---

• Golden Moment Rule #12 •

Veer Off the Beaten Path

*T*raveling entails both planning and a willingness to veer off the beaten
path. It's nice to visit the major tourist spots, but sometimes it's even
nicer to take a side trip and discover that what at first glance may seem
unremarkable suddenly becomes special once you are involved. So the
next time you plan a trip, allow yourself some time for a deeper exploration of an area. You may just stumble upon your own hidden treasure.

are mild. (It can be downright frigid in winter.) Enjoy the slower pace of days playing golf or biking the wide-open roads and beautiful vistas of this special island by the sea. Oh, and you'll eat really good lobster! For more information, contact www.gov.pe.ca/visitorsguide.

Let these destinations inspire you, excite you, and lead you to the vacation of your dreams. Now just do it! Choose it, plan it, and go for it!

A Final Note

The Gift of Travel

For me, traveling inspires a spirit of adventure. Adventure can be about testing your physical limits through activities, but it can also be about stretching your mind beyond what it is used to in everyday life. Family vacations require that you suspend your normal life and make a certain shift in attitude. What is that attitude, precisely? It's the attitude of being open to trying new things—a type of food, activity, or destination. On one of our family trips to Hawaii—in this case we were on the island of Kauai—my family and I were at the local fish shack, watching and waiting as the boats came into the dock with that day's fresh catch. The kids were jumping up and down, watching as some of the fish were still flopping on the docks, my husband was paying close attention to the fishing equipment the locals were cleaning on the boat, and I was taking in the moment. The sun was going down over the water, my family was all together, and we were just about to enjoy a glorious fresh meal.

Suddenly, movement across the street caught my attention: It was a line forming outside the Red Lobster restaurant. It was obvious most of the people in the line were tourists, and I thought to myself, "Wow, we're having so much more fun hanging and eating with the locals!"

Now, I have nothing against Red Lobster per se, but this choice of dining represents a missed opportunity; trying food in more intimate, indigenous surroundings will automatically change your perspective—on yourself, on eating fish, and on life in general. Isn't that why we travel in the first place?

I ask you, if we take vacations to get away from it all—work, school, worries, and the busy routine of life at home—then why wouldn't we step outside of what is familiar? This is how and why travel can be such a gift—not only for your children, but for you and your husband or partner, as well. Travel teaches us to look at our surroundings in a different way, experience the world in a different way, and as a result experience ourselves in a new, different, and often larger way. Children especially learn to expand their vision of the world, gain confidence as they meet the challenges presented by living outside of their normal routine, and develop understanding of other cultures, histories, and topographies. And when families travel together, we support and encourage one another as we try new sports, hike a mountain, or camp for the first time. Touring a beautiful countryside, biking the back roads of rural America, or discovering a secluded beach will be that much more meaningful if experienced with the ones we love. Indeed, vacation has that special power to bring families closer. So here's to your spirit of adventure! Break those internal boundaries and discover a part of yourself you never knew existed! Watch your kids grow in strength of mind, body, and spirit! And by all means, have fun!

Notes for Every Travel Mom

Use this space to keep track of your wish list for future family vacations, to record memories, and to document details that you can use for planning upcoming trips.

Family Vacation Wish List

Dream Destination: _____
_____

Ideal Timing: _____

Details for Planning: _____
_____
_____
_____
_____
_____
_____
_____
_____

Dream Destination: _____
_____

Ideal Timing: _____

Details for Planning: _____
_____
_____
_____
_____
_____
_____
_____
_____
_____

A Place for Memories

Destination: _____

_____

Flight Info: _____

_____

Budget: $ _____

Accommodations: _____

_____

_____

Restaurants: _____

_____

_____

What to Pack: _____

_____

_____

_____

_____

What Not to Pack: _____

_____

_____

_____

_____

Trip Highlights: _____

_____

_____

_____

_____

_____

_____

_____

_____

Notes for Every Travel Mom

Use this space to keep track of your wish list for future family vacations, to record memories, and to document details that you can use for planning upcoming trips.

Family Vacation Wish List

Dream Destination: _____

_____

Ideal Timing: _____

Details for Planning: _____

_____

_____

_____

_____

_____

_____

_____

_____

_____

Dream Destination: _____

_____

Ideal Timing: _____

Details for Planning: _____

_____

_____

_____

_____

_____

_____

_____

_____

A Place for Memories

Destination: _____

_____

Flight Info: _____

_____

Budget: $ _____

Accommodations: _____

_____

_____

Restaurants: _____

_____

_____

What to Pack: _____

_____

_____

_____

_____

What Not to Pack: _____

_____

_____

_____

_____

Trip Highlights: _____

_____

_____

_____

_____

_____

_____

_____

_____

Notes for Every Travel Mom

Use this space to keep track of your wish list for future family vacations, to record memories, and to document details that you can use for planning upcoming trips.

Family Vacation Wish List

Dream Destination: _____

_____

Ideal Timing: _____

Details for Planning: _____

_____

_____

_____

_____

_____

_____

_____

_____

Dream Destination: _____

_____

Ideal Timing: _____

Details for Planning: _____

_____

_____

_____

_____

_____

_____

_____

_____

A Place for Memories

Destination: _____
_____

Flight Info: _____
_____

Budget: $ _____
Accommodations: _____
_____
_____

Restaurants: _____
_____
_____

What to Pack: _____
_____
_____
_____
_____

What Not to Pack: _____
_____
_____
_____
_____

Trip Highlights: _____
_____
_____
_____
_____
_____
_____
_____
_____

Notes for Every Travel Mom

Use this space to keep track of your wish list for future family vacations, to record memories, and to document details that you can use for planning upcoming trips.

Family Vacation Wish List

Dream Destination: _____
_____

Ideal Timing: _____
Details for Planning: _____
_____
_____
_____
_____
_____
_____
_____
_____
_____

Dream Destination: _____
_____

Ideal Timing: _____
Details for Planning: _____
_____
_____
_____
_____
_____
_____
_____
_____
_____

A Place for Memories

Destination: _____

_____

Flight Info: _____

_____

Budget: $ _____

Accommodations: _____

_____

_____

Restaurants: _____

_____

_____

What to Pack: _____

_____

_____

_____

_____

What Not to Pack: _____

_____

_____

_____

_____

Trip Highlights: _____

_____

_____

_____

_____

_____

_____

_____

_____

Notes for Every Travel Mom

Use this space to keep track of your wish list for future family vacations, to record memories, and to document details that you can use for planning upcoming trips.

Family Vacation Wish List

Dream Destination: _____

_____

Ideal Timing: _____

Details for Planning: _____

_____

_____

_____

_____

_____

_____

_____

_____

Dream Destination: _____

_____

Ideal Timing: _____

Details for Planning: _____

_____

_____

_____

_____

_____

_____

_____

_____

_____

A Place for Memories

Destination: _____

_____

Flight Info: _____

_____

Budget: $ _____

Accommodations: _____

_____

_____

Restaurants: _____

_____

What to Pack: _____

_____

_____

_____

What Not to Pack: _____

_____

_____

_____

Trip Highlights: _____

_____

_____

_____

_____

_____

_____

_____

_____

Index

About the Author

Emily Kaufman, aka "the Travel Mom," is the travel contributor for ABC's *Good Morning America*. As one of the leading experts in family travel, she provides direction for all aspects from the perspective of a mom. In addition to *GMA*, she has appeared on *The View*, *Good Day Live*, and CNN. The Travel Mom is a regular contributor to *Woman's Day* magazine and hosts her own Web site at www.thetravelmom.com.

Mrs. Kaufman began her career on television as a parenting and family expert on shows such as *Mike and Maty* and *Crook & Chase*. She holds a degree from the University of Minnesota, where she studied early childhood development, speech communications, and child psychology. Emily combined her love of travel and her knowledge of parenting to become the Travel Mom.

In addition to her work as travel journalist, Emily offers her services as a corporate spokesperson. On behalf of these clients, the Travel Mom appears via television satellite, reaching millions of consumers. The Travel Mom can also be heard on radio around the country promoting various companies and destinations. She regularly appears as an expert speaker at travel industry functions and is the first resource that companies turn to for endorsement in the family travel arena.

Emily spends most of her time traveling the world in search of terrific family vacations. She is joined in this quest by her children, thirteen-year-old Gabby and fifteen-year-old Charlie. Her husband of fifteen years, Sid, tries to tag along whenever he can. She resides in Southern California but basically lives on a plane.